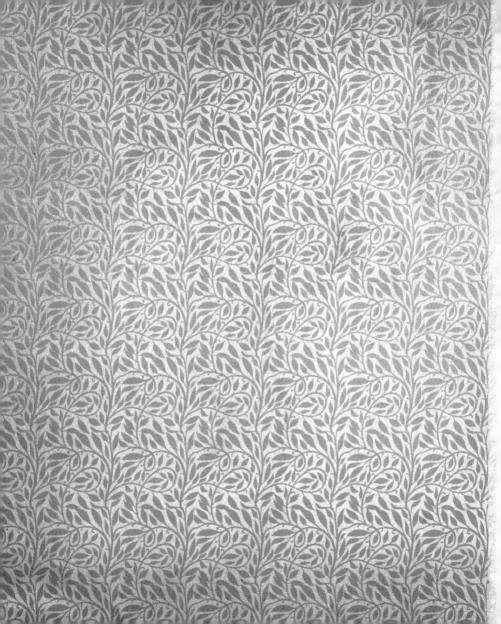

For Daddy

# Acknowledgments

As I wrote in *Legacy of Love: Things I Learned from My Mother*, I had the privilege of growing up around rather remarkable people.

I am deeply grateful for and indebted to:

My father: I am even more warmed by the embers than by the fire. His gentleness and grace color my world. This book is my tribute to him.

My mother, who has been the perfect life partner for my father and whose joy has always pervaded our home.

My siblings: Gigi, Anne, Franklin, and Ned, who share with me the legacy, joy, and responsibility of being Daddy's children.

There have been many contributors to this book, and I am so appreciative of them. I would like to give special thanks to:

All my honorary "aunts" and "uncles" who are/were part of the Billy Graham team. They have been like family—especially Uncle T. W. Wilson.

Russ Busby, who has followed my father around the world to chronicle his life and work in pictures. He is ever cheerful no matter how great the request!

My Aunt Virginia Somerville, who is a never-failing source of family history and who unearthed some of the never-before published photographs in this book.

David Bruce, who helped work behind the scenes to make sure this book was a surprise for Daddy.

John Akers, who read the manuscript with his keen eye for details and facts.

Stacy Mattingly, who helped to craft the book you now hold in your hand. This is our third book together, and my respect for her talent, her dogged pursuit of excellence, and her spiritual depth knows no bounds. She has taught me about the craft of writing and has become like a member of my family.

Sara Dormon, who continues to be my loyal friend, advisor, and executive administrator—she keeps me on track; and Anne Frank, my executive assistant, who brings joy whenever she comes through the door, as well as order to my desk.

Wes Yoder, my agent, for his friendship, guidance, and integrity; along with all the marvelous staff at Ambassador Agency. We have come a long way together.

Tom Dean, Associate Publisher of Inspirio, who first envisioned this book and has been an encourager all along the way—a delight to work with throughout. I would also like to thank the entire Inspirio team, whose persistence, creativity, and commitment to quality really show: Val Buick, Senior Vice President; Amy Wenger, Design Manager; and Kim Zeilstra, Editorial and Acquisitions Manager. Thank you for your attentiveness, long hours, and hard work. Thanks also to designer Chris Gilbert, whose skillfulness and diligence are reflected in the beauty of this book. A special thanks to Cindy Lambert, Director of Consumer Intelligence and Category

Strategy. I depend on her vision, professionalism, warmth, and insight, as well as her friendship.

Finally, in loving memory of my grandparents, Frank and Morrow Graham and Nelson and Virginia Bell. Their legacy lives on.

A Legacy of Faith
Copyright © 2006, 2014 by Ruth Graham

ISBN: 978-0-310-34474-2

Product Manager: Tom Dean
Design Manager: Amy Wenger
Production Manager: Matt Nolan
Design: studiogearbox.com

Printed in China
14 15 16 17 TIMS 5 4 3 2 1

# A Legacy of Faith

# A Legacy of Faith

THINGS I LEARNED *from* MY FATHER, BILLY GRAHAM

# RUTH GRAHAM

DAUGHTER *of* BILLY AND RUTH BELL GRAHAM

## *with* STACY MATTINGLY

## CHAPTER ONE

# Love for the World

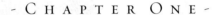

*For God so loved the world, that he gave his only begotten Son,*
*that whosoever believeth in him should not perish, but have everlasting life.*

JOHN 3:16 KJV

From the bay window in the kitchen, the mountains beyond the patch of lawn in front of our house look dismal and gray, partially shrouded by thick winter cloud cover. It is Saturday morning, just days before Christmas. Cold winds buffet the thick log walls of our home, Little Piney Cove, but the blazing fire in the kitchen fireplace holds off the chill. The house is abuzz with activity.

Refilling their coffee cups, Mother and Daddy urge my siblings and me to finish getting dressed. At eight years old, I do not need to be encouraged; eager for our departure, I am already layered in a turtleneck, thick sweater, and jacket. It is our annual "box delivery day," and soon my siblings and I will pile into the Jeep with our father to take gift boxes to some of the less fortunate mountain families who live in the vicinity of our village — Montreat, North Carolina.

In the kitchen, Mother — working with her secretary, Chris Jarrett, and our housekeeper, Bea Long — is still packing the boxes from our bountiful store: a table laden with an assortment of candy, fruit, meats, preserves, toys, and other Christmas gifts sent to our family by friends and associates. My siblings — sisters Gigi and Anne and brother Franklin (Ned is not yet a year old) — wander in one by one, and we hover around the table, watching closely as Mother chooses the items for each box.

We know better than to eye the table with longing. Mother and Daddy have schooled us in the business of giving. Gifts sent to our family are earmarked not for our own enjoyment, but for people in need. All too fresh in my memory is the beautiful soda fountain sent to Daddy after he appeared on the television program *This Is Your Life*. To my profound chagrin (I won't deny it!), the soda fountain went the way of other gifts we have received. In this case, the beneficiary was a ministry for young people on the streets of New York City.

As soon as Mother puts the finishing touches on the boxes, Daddy, aided by John Rickman, our longtime helper, carries them out to the Jeep, and my siblings and I follow, bundled in hats, scarves, coats, and boots. We climb into the Jeep, some of us holding the boxes in our laps, and wait for Daddy to crank up the engine. Taking the gearshift in one hand and the wheel in the other, he maneuvers us into position to descend our steep mountain drive. Then, in a moment, we're off!

Watching the pine trees go by, glancing at Daddy as he confidently navigates the winding driveway, my heart is full with expectation. My father is not at home much, and when he is home, his time is mostly consumed with meetings and the work of the ministry; so the free time he gets to spend with us always seems like a gift. On

ANNE, FRANKLIN, GIGI, AND ME (IN THE MIDDLE)

this particular day, not only do we get to be with Daddy, but we also get to help him in his capacity as "Reverend Graham," which is what the locals call him.

We sing Christmas carols as we pass the modest homes and the shacks set back into the hillsides. Taking the bumpy dirt roads with care, Daddy shares memories of Christmas on the dairy farm in Charlotte, North Carolina, where he grew up: the cows always had to be milked, but Mother Graham worked hard to make the day special. He also talks with us about what we are doing this morning, explaining that we are to be grateful for what God has given us, telling us the importance of sharing what we have with others, until finally we arrive at our first stop, a small, two-room cabin with a droopy front porch and wisps of smoke curling from a stone chimney.

At the sound of the leaves crunching under our wheels, several children peer out the cabin's front window. A man, their father, ambles out warily, a cap shading his face as he eyes us; and the children, dressed in ragged sweaters and mismatched boots, follow hesitantly behind.

Daddy quickly gets out of the Jeep and extends his hand, smiling and introducing himself. By this time the man has recognized my father; he tips his hat back, exposing a lined, leathery countenance, and takes Daddy's hand, shaking it firmly. The two men exchange a word or two; then Daddy motions for us to get out of the Jeep and bring one of the boxes.

Together my siblings and I walk over to the men and hand our father a gift box packed to overflowing. We smile politely. Not quite knowing what to do, we turn to the children and begin tossing a ball with them. I watch my father from a distance. Dressed in slacks, an Eisenhower jacket, and a gentleman's hat, he is handsome and tall, but not intimidating. He gazes at the man in front of him, leaning in close to listen. His gestures are open and warm. He nods. His face shows concern and understanding. Looking on, I feel intense pride. This is my father. He is a good man, a kind man. And I love him dearly.

Daddy puts his arm around the man's shoulder and they bow their heads for prayer. They shake hands again. The man moves back toward the cabin and Daddy toward the Jeep. For a moment they look at one another knowingly; then each calls his children to come on.

"Merry Christmas!" my siblings and I yell out to the children as we climb back into our vehicle. Starting the engine, Daddy turns to us and smiles. "Well," he says, "are you ready for the next house?"

## CALLED TO LOVE

Before anything else, my father is an evangelist. He lives to reach out to people, touch their lives for good, and help them find God. That is what he was made to do. Evangelism is his passion and his joy — he flourishes doing it.

For the fifty-plus years of my lifetime, I have never seen my father waver in his purpose. A forward-looking man driven by mission, he has maintained his focus sharing the gospel of Jesus Christ throughout years of overwhelming challenge, responsibility, and turmoil on the world stage. He has remained passionate, single-minded, and committed, even today, as his body slows down, leaving him limited mainly to our home in Montreat.

"The evangelistic harvest is always urgent," he wrote in his memoir, quoting his opening address at the 1966 World Congress on Evangelism in Berlin. "The destiny of men and of nations is always being decided. Every generation is crucial; every generation is strategic. But we are not responsible for the past generation, and we cannot bear full responsibility for the next one. However, we do have *our* generation! God will hold us responsible at the Judgment Seat of Christ for how well we fulfilled our responsibilities and took advantage of our opportunities."[1]

These are the words of a visionary, a man who knew he had a work to do, a man with his destiny in mind. In fact, his memoir, *Just As I Am*, took years to assemble, in part because my father was not convinced that spending his time looking *backward* would help him meet the pressing needs of his call. He is not inclined to ruminate; he doesn't want to be distracted from his mission; and in the case of his memoir, he did not presume that the world would be clamoring to read a book about his life and ministry, although he eventually conceded such a book could be helpful to others.

How does one explain the decades of resolute intensity that my father has applied to evangelism? What has kept him motivated? How has he sustained the level of passion and single-mindedness required to keep going, to keep dreaming, to keep planning? Re-reading some of the letters he wrote to my siblings and me from his evangelistic meetings around the world, I have begun to understand.

Here is the kind of observation we read in Daddy's letters so frequently, this one written from the 1969 meetings in Auckland, New Zealand:

> *As you all know, we were here in Auckland ten years ago for just a two-day crusade. I wish that you could see some of the results of that crusade. Last night a handsome young doctor and his lovely wife came*

to call on us just before the meeting. Ten years ago they had no church relationship and were totally outside of Christ. One evening they were reading the newspaper and read an account about our meetings. The wife said to her husband, "Let's go and see what this is all about." So out of sheer curiosity they came, and that night they were converted. Now they are two of the Christian leaders of Auckland. . . . Certainly this bears out the words of Isaiah, that God's Word "shall not return unto Me void, but it shall accomplish that which I please, and it shall prosper in the thing whereto I sent it."

And from the 1967 Tokyo meetings, he wrote:

It's very wonderful to watch the people night after night bringing their notebooks and writing down everything that I say. There is an earnestness and a sincerity to learn about Christ Jesus and the Christian way here that I have not witnessed in any other country. I have made the invitation to receive Christ extremely difficult, and an average of over a thousand has responded every night. For a Japanese to be converted it means a tremendous break with so much of everything he has ever known. Therefore, the Christians in Japan must be among the most devout and self-sacrificing to be found anywhere in the world.

In these passages, and in many others like them, I can see the essence of what drives my father, what has kept him determined to press ahead in ministry, to push forward, to expand, to do more, to give more of himself. It is the very thing I witnessed as a girl when we delivered Christmas boxes to the families living around Montreat. It is love. Love for God. Love for God's work in the lives of people. And love for the world. Not just love for the human family in general, not just for nations and cultures — but love for individuals. For that young doctor and his wife in Auckland. For the people in Japan listening attentively to his message and writing in their notebooks. For the North Carolina mountain man standing outside on a winter's day facing a difficult personal need. My father's gentle, sensitive heart opens for people, breaks for people, and, ultimately, longs for them to know the personal God from whom the greatest love comes.

The Bible says, "For God so loved the world, that he gave his only begotten Son" (John 3:16 KJV). As an evangelist, my father is called to extend that love — both with his words and with his life.

## Family Sacrifices

Sometimes my father's love for the world could be painful to me.

My father loves people intensely whether they are gathered en masse in a stadium or standing in front of him on the street. To the best of his ability, he makes time for people. As a child I never saw him express irritation toward anyone who might intrude on our privacy as a family in order to talk with him. I never saw him condescend to anyone. Our meals out together were frequently interrupted by people asking for autographs or wanting to share their personal struggles. Daddy was always very gracious, loving, and appreciative. He would stand to greet those who approached him, shake their hands, introduce us, and then listen.

I was not as generous in my heart when it came to sharing my father's time. He might not have resented the interruptions, but I must admit that I did. We had him at home with us so little — he estimates his long absences added up to about fifty or sixty percent of his life. And while I never doubted that my father loved me, often he was simply busy with someone else. I missed my father. I needed him. I needed his advice, his assurance, his affection, his encouragement — and, more than anything, I needed to be with him. But the unprecedented demands of his ministry required our family to make unique and difficult sacrifices.

I did not begrudge my father his work. I believed he was doing one of the most important jobs a person could do: sharing God's love through the gospel message. Mother constantly reinforced the significance of Daddy's ministry, telling us stories about people whose lives had been changed as a result. The adults close to us — my mother's parents, who lived at the bottom of our mountain; and retired missionaries who had settled in Montreat — frequently discussed reports from my father's meetings. Mother kept a globe in the kitchen so we could see where Daddy might be at any given time, and on Sundays, we would all gather around the radio to listen to *The Hour of Decision*, often broadcast from faraway places. "I'm Cliff Barrows," we would hear Daddy's close associate say, as he announced the program's location for that week, "and this is *The Hour of Decision!*"

Being a part of my father's ministry, at least peripherally, was a privilege, but, on some level, I think I grew up feeling that my personal needs had to be sublimated for the greater good. The world needed my father. God needed my father. Again, I knew Daddy loved me. I knew I was important to him. But I also knew there was something else "out there" — a great work, a calling to tell the world about the love of God. And I just couldn't compete with that.

"UNCLE CLIFF" BARROWS ON HIS WAY UP OUR MOUNTAIN, 1950S

Seeing Daddy off, Black Mountain, North Carolina, 1950s

## At Home

Mother did her best to mitigate the impact of my father's departures — perhaps for her own sanity as much as for ours — and we followed her lead. She simply didn't make a big deal out of his leaving. Taking Daddy to the train station in the nearby town of Black Mountain became an almost routine excursion. Mother never hung on to my father or cried and carried on when he left. She just kissed him, said good-bye, and we moved on to the next thing. Daddy was leaving to preach the gospel. That was his job. Meanwhile, I had homework waiting or dinner at my grandparents' house. Life went on. We didn't skip a beat. Mother got busy and began looking forward to my father's return, in the words of her adage, making "the most of all that comes and the least of all that goes."

In keeping with that same adage, Daddy's homecomings were a grand affair. Mother would generate a great deal of excitement as the date drew near for his return, and she would stage a celebration for his arrival. We would pile into the car, and she would drive us to the train station — this time to Old Fort, which is situated at a lower altitude than Black Mountain, in order to preempt the slow, uphill leg of the journey. We would meet up with friends and associates on the platform, making a contest out of who could spot the train first. And as the train pulled into the station, our crowd would

erupt with applause, shouting, and cheering. There was Daddy, descending the train, eagerly searching for us, the grin on his face growing wider when he spotted Mother.

Once we got home, my father would gather us into his bedroom while he unpacked the scarred, brown leather suitcases, handing out special gifts from the places he had visited. He would tell us stories about the people he had met — the tall Watutsis, the small Pygmies, the proud Masai, the Chinese who had endured imprisonment for their faith. Once he told me about the young daughter of a couple he had met in New Zealand, and she became my longtime pen pal.

My father spent as much time as he could with us when he was at home. He played with us and took us on long hikes; walking stick in hand, he would lead us, and a pack of dogs (all of them ours!), along the mountain ridges. One spring he took us to Sears, Roebuck and Co. in nearby Asheville. We brought home bags full of clothes, which Mother perused and then promptly returned. The sales clerk told her that she knew the items Daddy bought us were not exactly what we needed, but that he was having such a good time she didn't want to stop him.

Most days, my father spent long hours in his book-lined study reading, preparing for his next series of meetings, and dictating correspondence; and we made adjustments to keep the house quiet. We changed our phone number each time he came home — frustrating our childhood friends. And Mother discouraged us from having our friends over to visit during these periods. Many days we would arrive home from school to find cables stretched across the driveway, a sign that Daddy was taping *The Hour of Decision*, and we knew to keep the noise down. Daddy told me I was free to interrupt him at any time; he always made me feel wanted, and I knew I would be lovingly received. But I thought twice about interrupting my father. I don't think I ever did interrupt him when he was working in his office, no matter how urgent my problem seemed to me.

Perhaps this is where my frustration came into play toward those who took my father's time from us. People who didn't have a right to his time — especially those who, it appeared, just wanted to be seen with him — seemed to interrupt my father freely, while those of us who did have a right to his time, and to his love, refrained. It didn't seem fair. Our time together as a family was so limited. When a camera crew came to the house to shoot footage for *The World of Billy Graham*, they filmed several takes of us driving with Daddy along a mountain road in our convertible singing a song we had learned one summer in Switzerland; and I remember enjoying getting to be with my whole family — even if it was staged.

My father's absences had other painful consequences. One day when I was about eleven, I decided to visit a friend whose parents had rented a house on the local golf course. Daddy was an avid golfer and played whenever he had the chance, usually soon after he got home from ministry events. It was a way for him to relax.

This particular day, as my friend and I were outside playing in her yard under some trees that lined the fairway, I saw a group of golfers in the distance and recognized one of the men as my father. He was chatting with the others, and his familiar voice carried. Excited to have a surprise encounter with Daddy, I went out to greet him, but rather than welcome me, he waved his hand in the air to caution me. "Little girl," he called out, "you're going to be in danger — you need to move off the course!" He didn't recognize me. And I was too embarrassed to speak up.

Stories like this sadden Daddy. He has often expressed concern that he was not a good father to us when we were young, but that is simply not true — he loved us dearly. Being gone so much, he often lacked understanding about the dynamics at home; and he was not always able to lay the kind of groundwork in relationship with us that, perhaps, would have made relating to us easier. When tired, burdened with concerns, and faced with the demands of fathering five rough-and-tumble children (we could be a wild bunch), he became short-tempered at times. But we learned to give him latitude. Mother taught us to let things go and "know Daddy's heart." And I knew my father's heart — it was full of love.

SAYING GOODBYE: DADDY, MOTHER, AND ME

## Keeping it Real

Though many of my father's trips would last for months at a time, I did not grow up conscious of the magnitude of Daddy's fame and position. We never talked about his work in those terms. I knew he was a preacher who traveled. I understood his work was extremely important. But outside of his being my daddy, I did not think of him as a celebrity. I remember being impressed when his close associate George Beverly Shea came to visit us in Florida one winter. I thought, "Now here's a really famous person!"

My parents worked hard to help us maintain a down-to-earth view of my father and his ministry. They kept it real, doing their best to give us a normal upbringing out of the limelight so that we would have a healthy perspective on the world and our place in it. Mother and Daddy did not think of themselves as entitled. I never picked up on any sense from them that our family was owed special treatment because of the ministry. My parents simply did not think like that. It was God, not my father, who deserved attention and accolades.

Perhaps the most important decision my parents made was to bring us up in the unassuming mountain community of Montreat. Many of the citizens—like my grandparents, who spent nearly twenty-five years in China—were retired missionaries and pastors who had traveled the world, so the nature of my father's work did not seem unusual. The adults in Montreat treated us like normal children, and if they saw us misbehaving they did not gossip, but prayed for us instead. No one in Montreat ever told me that I had to live up to a particular standard just because I was Billy Graham's child.

We did know that my father's ministry was impacting people around the world. Mother traveled to Europe. Daddy's assistants and associates, our honorary "aunts" and "uncles," traveled with him. We knew our parents had tea with the Queen of England. I can remember my father golfing with President-elect John F. Kennedy. When he was vice president, Richard Nixon came to our home (I was not present). And we certainly heard about my father's interactions with dignitaries and heads of state, frequently seeing pictures of these meetings in the newspaper. But my parents did not make a big deal over their relationships with people of influence. These relationships, though valued by Mother and Daddy, were accepted as part of the work of the ministry and viewed with the understanding that God alone deserved our highest regard, not people, be they famous or otherwise.

Mother used to say that Daddy taking his family to his evangelistic meetings was like a general taking his family to battle, so we attended very few of my father's crusades as we were growing up. I remember going to the 1957 New York crusade at age six and being overwhelmed by the enormous crowds. Later, as a teenager, I attended the 1966 and '67 London meetings. We would arrive at each night's event by car with Mother or a staff person and park in a designated area. Though we remained anonymous, we sat in special seating, often with special guests, and prayed for those around us when Daddy gave the invitation. I loved the excitement, but it was only after I got married that I traveled to my father's meetings with any regularity, sometimes working as a counselor; at other times sitting anonymously in the crowd to support and pray for those going forward to receive Christ.

My father did try to include us in his work in other ways. He wrote us wonderful letters — individual and group letters — from wherever he happened to be preaching, giving us a window into his world.

"It is wonderful to be back in London again, seeing so many old friends and seeing so many people that received Christ when we were here last June," he wrote in 1966, before I joined him for the crusade in that city. "Last night the Royal Albert Hall, seating nearly 7,000 was packed to capacity with the converts of last June's Crusade. What a thrilling, joyous sight. How they sang! While I was preaching the Word to them I felt like they were little birds in the nest opening their mouths and taking in the food that was being offered."

In a quick handwritten note jotted to me from Switzerland weeks later, Daddy, as he often did, asked me to pray for the work: "We are on the way to Berlin for a Crusade that begins on Oct. 16," he wrote, "and a World Congress on Evangelism that begins on Oct. 25 — Please pray for both these important events."

Days later, from Berlin, Daddy set down this description of a haunting incident, allowing us to see with his eyes:

> Then we had an experience I'll never forget. We went to the British sector and stood upon the platform looking over the wall into East Germany. The wind was biting cold. Immediately the Communist guards shined their spotlights in our faces and began to shoot off rockets to frighten us. We stood there for about ten or fifteen minutes watching this terrible sight: The wall, the mine fields, the barbed wire, etc. I certainly feel sorry for the people of Berlin. There are so many divided families that can never be reunited because of this terrible wall.

Here was the love again, coming out in Daddy's letter — his

love for people; his love for the world; for the oppressed; the hurting; the lonely and desolate. That love seemed to touch my father's every observation. And he brought us into the love — into his heart. We might not get to be with him in person, but through his efforts to reach out, we could enter his perspective, as if we were standing there on the platform looking out over the wall with him, watching the rockets fire into the air, mourning the mines and the barbed wire, and sharing his love for those divided families in Berlin.

## EXPERIENCING THE LOVE

Occasionally, my father did bring us with him into smaller ministry settings. I got to travel with him as his special guest on a few trips, and while I did not spend much one-on-one time with him at the events, just being part of his world and watching him in action made me feel included. He was always gracious in the way he treated me, greeting me with a smile, hug, and kiss; introducing me to the people we met along the way. Ever the gentleman, he made me feel the lady.

When I was thirteen, he took me to the World's Fair in New York City for what I remember was Billy Graham Day; he and a crew from World Wide Pictures, the filmmaking arm of the Billy Graham Evangelistic Association (BGEA), had arranged a special makeup session and photo shoot for me. Holding my hand as we walked the fairgrounds, my father looked down at me and said, "People are going to wonder why I am holding hands with such a beautiful blonde!" I blushed, but I felt so grown-up and proud to be with him. My father's affection built my confidence like nothing else.

Perhaps most significantly for me, when I was ten Daddy took me to a revival at a Baptist church in Florida, where our family was wintering that year. My father's associate Lee Fisher was holding the revival in a nearby city, and Daddy attended in order to lend support. The sanctuary was small, and we slipped into one of the pews in back so as not to draw too much attention.

Near the end of the service, Mr. Fisher ("Uncle Lee," as we called him) invited people who wished to make a public confession for Christ to come forward. The pianist was playing a hymn, and I remember feeling self-conscious standing at my seat. I wanted to go forward, but what would people think? I was already conspicuous in the little church — despite his best efforts my father drew attention wherever he went — and I did not want to make more of a scene by going to the altar. What if I embarrassed my father? I dreaded being noticed.

But whatever my fears, they passed quickly. The "yes" to go

forward became stronger than the "no" holding me back. Overcoming the awkwardness, I walked to the front of the church and stood before Uncle Lee with my eyes shut tight and my head down. I could hear movement and the sound of footsteps — other people coming forward. Then, suddenly, I felt a hand on my shoulder. I opened my eyes and recognized my father's hand. He was standing with me there in front of the congregation. The evangelist who had invited countless people around the world to commit their lives to Christ now stood with me, his daughter, as I responded and made that same public commitment. This was how my father so often had loved the world — and now he was showing that same love to me, in the most intimate way.

ME, AGE 13

## SHOWING ME THE WAY

Jesus said, "By this all men will know that you are My disciples, if you have love for one another" (John 13:35 NASB). Over the course of my lifetime, I have watched my father's love for others steadily deepen. Even now, spending most of his time in our home, he remains riveted to world affairs, constantly reading, staying current on news, and searching for ways to get help to those who need it. My father's love has always gone beyond preaching the gospel. As he showed me in childhood when delivering goods to the needy at Christmastime, his heart is to love the whole person, and that includes meeting practical needs.

Most recently, the effects of the December 2004 tsunami in Asia and Hurricane Katrina, which wiped out New Orleans and devastated the Gulf Coast in August 2005, have consumed my father. He spent hours in front of the television watching coverage of these disasters, talking of little else, and working with the BGEA World Relief Fund — and my brother Franklin, president of the relief organization Samaritan's Purse — to come up with strategies for supporting the victims. I know my father feels discouraged that he can't be on the front lines helping in a hands-on way, as he would have done in years past.

Seeing his frustration, I remembered something Daddy's mother once said in an interview. "He didn't know how to say no," Mother Graham explained, referring to the many speaking invitations he received as a young man. In her words, Daddy was "always willing." Always ready to pick up and meet people's needs. That's my father — driven by love, driven to help, saying "yes" as often as he can.

Ultimately, I think, what my father has demonstrated throughout a lifetime of ministry is a commitment to love others to the point of self-sacrifice. He sacrificed his privacy, personal time, and relationships; and the work took a great toll on his body. Though it was my father's desire to say "yes" and give whatever God required of him, giving as he did wasn't easy. We sacrificed a lot in his absence — but so did he.

"For myself," he wrote in his memoir, "as I look back, I now know that I came through those years much the poorer both psychologically and emotionally. I missed so much by not being home to see the children grow and develop…. Our children could not possibly have missed their daddy nearly as much as I missed them and their mother when I was away."[2]

My father has set a high standard in giving himself wholeheartedly; I have sought more of a balance and tend to be more restrained. It may be that seeing my father give so much to others when I was a child caused me to become reserved in loving. I think I felt that he gave away so much of what was mine — attention, concern, love, and time — that I became protective of my heart. I was not willing to give everything away.

My reserve may be partly a function of my personality. I'm slower to engage others, more of an observer than a participant. Still, while learning to love in a way uniquely my own, I try to draw on my father's example. I would like to be more present with people — to respond in love to those who cross my path at an airport or restaurant; to reach out to the elderly, the needy, the forgotten. I regularly pray for a tender heart, a greater capacity to encourage others, and a willingness to be inconvenienced. Pictures of this kind of love, I realize, are my father's gifts to me. He has shown me the way, and whatever childhood hurts I might have experienced due to his absences, I am privileged to have as a father such a man — a kind, committed man who loves without holding back. A man who has sought to love the way God loves, so the world could recognize that love — and reach for it.

PREACHING IN A BAHAMIAN CHURCH, 1986

PAR AVION

Daddy in India with victims of a cyclone and tidal wave, 1977

- C H A P T E R  T W O -

# A Father's Heart

*Fathers tell their children about your faithfulness.*

ISAIAH 38:19 NIV

Chicago, 1971. It is the last night of my father's crusade at the McCormick Place arena and I am hurrying to Daddy's hotel room, hoping to see him before the night's event begins. I have never done this before — gone to see my father in the middle of his preparation time at a crusade. But I am feeling a little desperate. Newly married and just twenty, I have been arguing with my husband. I need some kind of assurance — assurance that I am loved, I suppose. I have no idea if my father will have time for me. Or what he might say. Or what I even need him to say. All I know is that I want his comfort.

Answering my knock, Daddy's longtime associate and friend T. W. Wilson — "Uncle T" — opens the door to a room adjoining my father's. A tall, heavy-set man, Uncle T smiles warmly and seems delighted to see me. Fiercely loyal to my parents, he has treated my siblings and me like his own, and he always makes me feel important.

"Can I see Daddy?" I ask now, trying to hide my desperation. Uncle T looks into my eyes, tilting his head to the side as if he understands. He puts his arm around me and motions toward the door separating us from Daddy.

"Go ahead," he says. "He's in there."

I cross the room and peer through the crack in the door, which is slightly ajar. Even though I am about to interrupt my father, I don't feel nervous — just anxious, hoping he can spare a minute for me. I see him sitting across the room on the bed. Hearing me, he looks up and smiles.

"Come in, Bunny. Come in."

Always the Southern gentleman, Daddy stands as I enter, letting his papers drop and leaving a deep indentation in the pillows propped against the headboard. The shades in his room are drawn as usual. His large brown suitcase sits open on the opposite bed, and in his open briefcase on the floor beside him I see a pile of books, files, and paperwork. He is already dressed for the evening in suit pants and a dress shirt.

"Daddy, I'm sorry to interrupt," I start, "but it's just that … I …" Fumbling over my words, I feel the tears start to come.

"What's wrong?" my father asks, stepping forward and putting his arms around me. I stand there for a few seconds resting my head on his shoulder, trying to collect myself so I can tell him what's bothering me. Then I explain what happened with my husband.

"How do I deal with this?" I ask.

Sitting back down on the bed, Daddy motions for me to sit next to him. "Bunny," he says, speaking gently, but firmly, as if to cut through the emotion of the moment, "I know it can be difficult when you are newly married, and both of you are young. But the way I can answer you is to say that your mother let me know early on that she is married to Christ first. She does not depend on me to fulfill all of her needs. And regardless of what happens during the day, your mother always kisses me good night and tells me she loves me."

## DEPENDING ON GOD

This encounter with my father sticks in my mind for several reasons. Not only was it one of the only instances I can recall interrupting him, but it was also one of the few times I went to my father with a problem. As the middle of five children, I tended to avoid rocking the boat. Beyond that, I simply did not want to distract Daddy from his work. As a result, I often kept my struggles to myself; so, on this occasion when I did reach out for my father, to have him respond to me despite his pressing responsibilities spoke volumes.

But it is the advice he gave that really strikes me. At the time I didn't quite understand what my father was getting at. What he said actually caught me off guard. I think I wanted him to indulge my self-pity and take my side against my husband. He did neither. His advice called me out of self-pity. It pointed me to Christ and his design for healthy relationships. It forced me to look at myself, not just at my husband, and take responsibility for my own attitude. My father's advice was characteristically simple, yet profound and correct. Like Mother, I was to depend on Christ to meet my needs and the rest would follow.

What Daddy said about Mother being "married to Christ first" also reflected his own approach to life and ministry. Due to the magnitude of his calling, he had to believe with full conviction that he was not responsible for all of Mother's needs — or for all of ours. During long absences my father had to trust God with our well-being. He prayed for us constantly, followed God's direction as best he could, and trusted God — and Mother — to cover what he missed. That was how he had to live. Thankfully, his forward-looking outlook on life kept him from dwelling on the problems, challenges, and failures. Instead, my father's relentless drive to keep going forced him to keep depending on God. With so much on his plate he had no other choice. In God's care is where he had to leave us.

MOTHER AND DADDY
AT HOME, 2005

## FATHERING FROM A DISTANCE

Leaving us in God's hands was what my father had to do; but as I've shared, he missed out on a lot, and he knew it. In a group letter to my siblings and me from Auckland, New Zealand, when I was in college, he wrote, wistfully, "I wish we could turn the clock back for a few years just for an hour or two so that all of us could be together once again. I'd love to hear you laugh, or cry — or even fight!"

In another letter, sent to me some months after my marriage and referencing a very honest letter I had written to him, my father replied: "I really appreciate you writing the way you did — I hope you always feel free to do so. It means so much to me especially since I was away from home so much when you were growing up — and have felt my inadequacy as a father. When you say you love me and are proud of me that makes me feel really great! I love you with all my heart and am proud of you."

And yet, whatever his limitations, Daddy did a great deal to father us from a distance and work around his schedule. He visited us at our respective schools whenever he could. (Once he and Uncle T came to the boarding school I attended in Florida with Uncle T's daughter, Sally, and took us away for a father-daughter weekend.) My father also commissioned "surrogates." My future in-laws, for example, Fred and Millie Dienert, regularly took me to dinner or shopping in New York City while I was attending boarding school on Long Island. I also have at least one letter in which my father asked a colleague to introduce himself to me when he next visited my college and to invite me to spend a Sunday with his family. "She would love it," Daddy urged.

Of course, all of Daddy's close associates were like parents to us. Cliff Barrows and Uncle T wrote me beautiful, supportive letters when I got engaged at eighteen. Uncle T wrote, "It is hard to realize that you are a grown woman now. But, you are just as sweet now as the cute baby that we once knew. We love you for what you are: yourself, unaffected by your dad's fame, your disposition, charm, and real warmth." These were the kind, encouraging words of someone who loved me like his own.

And once Daddy even commissioned *me* as a kind of surrogate to look after my younger brother, Franklin. My brother and I were spending the summer in Israel helping with the World Wide Pictures film, *His Land*. Daddy was in New York City for his 1969 crusade, and he wrote to me with some urgency, stressing his conviction that the summer represented a pivotal time in Franklin's life. "I believe this is <u>why God has you in Israel</u> ... to be of help to Franklin," my father wrote. "... [L]ove him a lot — listen to him — pull him out — on spiritual things and on his life's work ... there is a limit to what I can do — <u>but you can do a lot</u>."

IN JERUSALEM: ANNE, GIGI, FRANKLIN, MOTHER, AND ME, 1960

Though my father often could not reach out to us in person, the truth is he did much effective parenting through phone calls, telegrams, and letters. Mother clued him in on our needs so that he could step in and provide comfort, direction, support, caution, or reprimand. The following are some of the areas in which he extended himself to me.

### Love and Affection

My father has always known how to show love. He is gentle and affectionate, never hesitating to tell me how much he loves me, emphasizing how often he thinks of and prays for me; and these traits come out so clearly in his letters. Here are some of his typical sign-offs in letters written either to me or to my siblings and me as a group:

~ *With a heartfelt love for each one of you in your particular place. Daddy*

~ *With Much Affection Your Adoring Daddy*

~ *I love You and Am Proud of You Daddy*

~ *With a heart full of love and pride, I am Affectionately yours, Daddy*

~ *With much love and affection, and many kisses, DADDY*

~ *Adoringly yours, Daddy*

In a letter he wrote to me during a very difficult year I spent at boarding school in New York, he expressed his concern with tenderness: "My dearest Bunny: I have just been talking to you over the phone. Naturally I sensed something of the burden of your heart. I wish it had been possible for me to be there and put my arms around you and tell you how much I love you — and how proud I am of you! I hope you will always know that your mother and father love you more than any other two people in the world and want to do what is best for you."

My father sent me many letters during that trying year at school. At the beginning of my junior year, he and Mother had enrolled me at the school in New York — a change from the comparatively tropical environs I had known at my previous school in Florida — and I had contracted mononucleosis. The transition was tough. I battled dread daily and was terribly homesick.

"I am sure that Bunny is going to need all of our prayers in a very special way," Daddy wrote in a group letter to my siblings and me from London as I was beginning the fall semester. "This mononucleosis is still holding on, and … leads to depression and physical weakness. However, I am sure that Bunny is going to be a ray of sunlight at that school and be a great help to the faculty in witnessing to the other students."

My father always addressed me during this period in an upbeat, encouraging way, dropping me postcards and letters to remind me of the hope on the other side of sickness and loneliness. He expressed sympathy. He let me know that he was standing with me in my battle. But, as in the scene in his Chicago hotel after my argument with my husband, he would not let me wallow in self-pity or get bogged down in emotions. He called me to higher ground, urging me to keep my chin up and see beyond the problem. His encouragement pointed to spiritual values: the development of Christian character and reliance on the Scriptures for guidance.

"I'm terribly distressed to hear you are not feeling well," he wrote from Switzerland, " — be sure I'm praying for you every day. … I'm certain it has been a big adjustment for you — and it will take at least 3 or 4 months to get used to it. However I believe it will … make you into a stronger Christian if you stick it out. <u>We are all proud of you</u>."

Part of the way my father encouraged me was to let me know how he saw me, regardless of what I might feel about myself. These observations carried weight — to know my father saw value in me at such a low time gave me the hope I needed to persevere.

"Just a brief note from here in Florida to let you know that I am thinking of you constantly and thank God that I have such a wonderful daughter," he wrote near the close of the fall semester. "Really, I have been proud of you this year more than any other year. I know the adjustments have been extremely difficult and yet you have acted like a faithful soldier. The real, true Bunny is coming out. In times of difficulties, disappointment, and crisis, she has courage, faith, conviction, poise, and love. For all of this that we see in you, we are thankful and proud."

## Spiritual Guidance

My father did more than just share his love for me in words; he backed up his declarations with practical guidance. In one letter Daddy sent to me that year in New York, he laid out extensive spiritual direction and an assortment of Scriptures, giving me principles that I could take away and apply.

> There are two little words that I have used time after time when I have faced problems, dilemmas, and even the devil. They are: "Fear not." Someone has said that they are "the divine hush for God's children."
>
> All of us face problems in our lives when we need the divine hush. To Abraham God said: "Fear not, I am thy shield and thy exceeding great reward" (Genesis 15:1); and to Joshua: "Fear not, neither be thou dismayed" (Joshua 8:1); and to Gideon: "Peace be unto thee; fear not, thou shalt not die" (Judges 6:23). How often we think we would rather be dead than to have to go through with our problems and difficulties, yet God promises, "Fear not, thou shalt not die."
>
> Then again: "Fear not, for they that be with us are more than they that be with them" (2 Kings 6:16). Now the devil is going to try to get you down a thousand times. He is going to work every angle. He is an old and experienced hand at discouragement, despondency, and especially in trying to sidetrack young people. But remember:

AT HOME: ANNE, MOTHER, GIGI, FRANKLIN, DADDY, AND ME (LEANING ON MOTHER)

*"They that be with us are more than they that be with them."*

*Remember Psalm 23:4: "I will fear no evil for Thou art with me."
Or remember Psalm 27:1: "The Lord is my light and my salvation; whom
shall I fear?" Or again the Psalmist said: "The Lord is at my side, I will
not fear what man can do unto me."...*

*Remember, dear Bunny — we love you, but God loves you even
more! Even while you are sleeping, He is at work on your problem.*

Looking back at these words, I can see the dimensions of my
father's heart. I see his trust in God to sustain him in all circumstances. I see his complete dependence on the truth of God's Word.
I see his determination to stay the course, to remain focused on his
purpose, and to fend off fear and distraction, which he must have
had to do constantly. And, again, I see the way he looked to God
to protect and care for those he loved. "God loves you even more!"
he wrote. God was taking care of me while I slept. Perhaps in writing these things, he was also encouraging himself in faith. God was
looking after his family. "Fear not."

## MEDIATED RELATIONSHIP

I remember the first time I went out somewhere to meet my
father on my own. It was the summer of 1965. At fourteen, I had
traveled to New York City by myself to visit a family friend. Mother

had phoned last minute to let me know Daddy was in the city too, having had a sudden change of plans. She gave me the name of his hotel and told me to go see him as soon as I could.

I found the hotel easily. Leaving my friend in the lobby, I boarded an elevator and punched the number for Daddy's floor. I felt exhilarated. There I was, not yet fifteen, on my own in a big city, and venturing out to meet my father. I felt independent and very adult; maybe a little reticent about intruding on him, but pleased that our lives were intersecting apart from the usual ways.

Once on Daddy's floor, I followed the signs to the room number Mother had given me and rapped gently on the door. A man I did not recognize answered.

"Can I help you?" he asked, looking at me, a young, blond teenager, with a little bemusement.

"Yes," I said, smoothing my dress. "I would like to see Mr. Graham." I'm not sure why I didn't just ask outright to see my father. Maybe it threw me not to see someone familiar, like Uncle T, answering the door. Maybe I thought I had gotten the room number wrong. In any case, the man told me Daddy was unavailable.

"I'm sorry," he said, closing the door. "That won't be possible. But have a wonderful day."

I looked at the man as he disappeared behind the door, leaving me standing there in the quiet hallway. I figured my father was probably busy anyway. Besides, I hadn't told the man I was Mr. Graham's daughter, so what was I to expect? How was he to know? Deflated, I turned and followed the corridor back to the elevator.

As I reached out to punch the elevator button on the wall, I heard a door open and close down the hall behind me. Then I heard a man's voice: "Wait!"

Looking around, I saw it was the man from Daddy's room. "Are you Bunny?" he asked apologetically. "Please come with me. I'm so sorry. Your father wants to see you right away."

The man who came after me that day at the New York hotel immediately ushered me into Daddy's room, thus averting a misunderstanding. But in actuality I was accustomed to obstacles when it came to gaining access to my father.

Born at the end of 1950, more than a year after Daddy's ministry had achieved national prominence in Los Angeles, I suppose I never really knew what it was like to have regular access to him. Gradually, as I got older and the ministry continued to expand, the experience of a largely mediated relationship with my father became normal. I simply had to go through someone else to get to Daddy. That was our reality.

I did feel frustrated on some level with the way things were, but, ultimately, I must have gotten used to it. At times I actually found it easier to go to a staff member and say, "This is what I need," rather than make the often exhausting effort to get to my father myself. Plus, I loved the staff with all of my heart. They were wonderful men and women of God—solid, loving, honorable people who would have gone to battle to protect my siblings and me.

But though I lived surrounded by people of the highest caliber, though I adapted to the peculiar dynamics of home life in the midst of a global ministry, the reality remained that my relationship with my father was often a mediated one. Mother, for example, lovingly called Uncle T her "husband-in-law," since he was frequently just in the next room. We adored the people who gave their lives to support and care for us, and I am grateful to them beyond my ability to express. But nothing changed the fact that we were hardly ever alone as a family, and that I could not easily get to my own father.

ME WITH DADDY'S SECRETARY, "AUNT LUVERNE" GUSTAVSON

## Hole in my Heart

The difficulty of the "mediated" dynamic began to surface once I became a teenager. I was beginning to face decisions and choices that would affect the course of my life, and I needed my father's advice. I needed him to sit down with me and help me evaluate my strengths and weaknesses. I wanted his input on what direction my life should take. Daddy did his best, but in spite of his efforts to reach out to me through the limited means available to him, in spite of his constant assurances of love, our mediated relationship during these critical years at times took a toll on my heart.

Sometimes it was simply Daddy's exhaustion or the burdens of ministry that forestalled the kind of involvement I needed from him. I remember being on a family trip in California not long before I was to graduate from high school. One afternoon some of us were sitting in the family room, and the subject of what I would do next in life came up. Daddy was about to go back to his bedroom to rest when I mentioned that I wanted to enroll in a nursing program at Wheaton College, my parents' alma mater. My father's face immediately grew taut, taking on an expression I recognized, and he looked at me steely-eyed. "No," he said flatly. And that was the end of the discussion. When Daddy got tired or frustrated about something, he could make a decree and that would be the end of it.

These instances were not the norm with my father; he worked very hard to give me as much of himself as he could. And when he was unavailable, we were fortunate to be surrounded by honorable men who could step in to help. Looking back, I see that these beloved "uncles" were part of the way God himself provided support for me in the absence of my father. These loving staff members were not just my father's surrogates; they were people sent by God to help me during my important, formative years. God, after all, knew what he had called my father to do. He knew my father's heart and prayers for us. And he knew what we would need in Daddy's absence to grow into the people we were called to be.

And yet, even with the support of both my father and my "uncles," I did have a hole in my heart due to the long separations from Daddy. My choice to get married at eighteen was probably my way of trying to fill that hole. My father didn't want me to marry so young. He strongly urged me to finish college first. I now wonder if my stubbornness in proceeding with the wedding, despite Daddy's reservations (though he certainly gave our marriage his support), was the fruit of the distance I felt from him. At the time of my engagement, I was ready to feel significant to someone. Perhaps I didn't really believe my father knew me — my heart and my needs — and, therefore, I resisted his sound judgment and reasoning.

On some level too, I think, the distance in my relationship with my father caused me to see God, my heavenly Father, as being similarly removed from my day-to-day life and intimate needs. As with Daddy, I knew that God loved me, but I also believed he was "busy with someone else." It took years of purposeful effort to change my view of God as One who loved from a distance. I had to learn how to be close to God, and I had to learn to trust in his closeness to me. In my thirties, I led a Bible study called "Enjoying God" that helped me break down these barriers. Finally, I was able to see that God wasn't too busy — that he always had time for me and was always nearby. Understanding this in turn helped me to better appreciate my own father's unconditional love for me. I had chafed at his absences and his preoccupation with ministry; now, in my adult years, I was beginning to see just how deep his love for me had run.

You might say that my relationship with Daddy resembles a mosaic of purposeful visits, correspondence, phone calls, and mediated communication, with the mode of our connection gradually flexing and adapting to suit the evermore pressing needs of the ministry. I don't think I noticed our relationship becoming increasingly mediated while it was happening; nor did I notice the effect the ministry's expansion had on our family while I was living in the midst of the change. Looking back now, though, I see that our young family eventually splintered, in some sense becoming more a collection of parts than a whole. We consisted of a father who was out fulfilling his ministry, a mother at home fulfilling her ministry (which by no means undermines her committed, vital partnership with my father), and five children going their separate ways, first to school and, eventually, to raise their families and fulfill ministries of their own.

While Mother and Daddy worked hard to preserve a sense of unity among us, and while God gave us all grace to handle the separation from one another, we still faced serious challenges as a family. I longed for a closeness and level of communication we simply could not sustain. That was one of the costs of Daddy's calling. It didn't make his heart toward us any less passionate or devoted, but it was a cost.

## Knowing My Father's Heart

Though I left school at eighteen to get married, I promised my father I would eventually go back. I never forgot that promise, or Daddy's desire to see me complete my education; and at forty, after my marriage broke down, I decided to pick up the books once again. Over the next decade I studied in fits and starts, finally earning my undergraduate degree in religion and communications from Mary Baldwin College in Virginia's Shenandoah Valley. I received my diploma in May 2000, a half-year shy of my fiftieth birthday.

Both of my parents, at great physical cost, came to Virginia for my commencement, as did my oldest sister, Gigi. Daddy stood at the podium that bright May morning and gave the benediction for my graduating class. Later, at a luncheon given by my children, he asked his associates to bring in a large, awkwardly wrapped gift. He made a big deal over it and wanted everyone to watch as I unwrapped it. Underneath the paper was a life-sized, glazed ceramic sculpture of a Boxer dog. "Because you worked like a dog," he said, smiling from where he sat by Mother in a corner chair. I was tickled and learned that, at eighty-one, he had actually gone shopping for this quirky gift himself!

Several aspects of my relationship with my father came to the surface on graduation weekend. First, in even attending, Daddy made a real effort to see me in person, as he has done from my boarding-school days. Further, in offering the benediction and sharing himself with the Mary Baldwin community, he reached out and touched others while supporting me — he extended love to those in *my* world. Then, in front of my friends and loved ones, my father openly expressed his affection for me, acknowledging the long road I had traveled to achieve a personal goal. He was proud and unashamedly loving as always.

At the same time, behind the scenes, getting my father to my graduation was, characteristically, something of an ordeal. Even securing his participation involved a slew of phone calls between my sister Gigi, his staff, and me; and due to health reasons, he was almost unable to come. I had no direct communication with Daddy until I insisted — of course, third-party communication has been our status quo for years. And yet, while I struggled with the familiar dynamic; ultimately, behind the confusion and drawn-out effort, I saw my father's heart. He exerted himself to be with me at an important moment and played his role as a proud father, celebrating my achievement. I needed him, and he tackled the challenges to come through. I will never forget that. Those memories of him are mine to cherish.

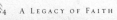

In all, despite the challenges of my father's ministry, despite the losses and sacrifices, despite the loneliness and hurt that often resulted from not having my father around more often, I have led a rich, interesting life as a Graham. I grew up around remarkable people and was privy to thought-provoking perspectives on the events of my day. I had opportunities to travel abroad from a very young age — to Europe, and, notably, to Japan and Korea with my grandparents, Nelson and Virginia Bell. Later I traveled to Africa and the Middle East. And Mother grew up in China, so we were exposed to different cultures and ways of seeing the world from our earliest days.

But I think the most important benefit of having grown up around my father's ministry is that of being the child of my father. Though we have weathered storms — or, perhaps, *because* we have weathered storms — I feel closer to him now than ever before. When I go home to Montreat, the house teems with caregivers who tend to my parents, both in their eighties. My father spends a lot of time resting and reading, but I still get to steal precious time alone with him.

I might be sitting in the kitchen early in the morning reading the newspaper and sipping coffee, relaxing in one of the overstuffed chairs by the bay window; and Daddy will come in, moving slowly with his walker. I will get up to greet him, exchange a hug and kiss, and go to the coffee pot to pour him a cup of weak coffee, as he takes a seat at the table.

At times like this, when it is just the two of us, unhurried, my father will talk with me about what is on his heart. Something he notices in one of the newspapers might spark conversation. Or maybe something he has been thinking about for days will come up. I know that if I press my father with questions, he will more than likely shut down — so many people ask him questions that he is often put off by it at home. But if I wait for him to talk to me on his terms, eventually he will begin. He is a quiet, thoughtful man and, like most men, will open up in his own time. If I listen, I will hear my father's heart. And that is what I long for most of all.

DADDY AND ME AT HOME, 1993

# ~ CHAPTER THREE ~

# *Humility*

*I have become all things to all men,*

*so that I may by all means save some.*

1 Corinthians 9:22 NASB

Not many years ago, Daddy placed a call to one of my sister Gigi's friends whom he had met previously. Getting the friend on the line, my father began the conversation this way: "Hello. This is Billy Graham. Do you remember me?"

I love this anecdote. It illustrates who my father really is — a man who doesn't think of himself as any more important than the next person. Not that he is naïve about his influence in the world. He simply doesn't presume others know him or think him exceptional.

If I had to name the one overriding character trait that I see in my father, it would be humility. Daddy, I am sure, would object. But I have watched my father's humility operate consistently and on many levels throughout my lifetime. I am constantly touched by the modest way he expresses himself. He is unassuming, even when caught by surprise, which shows his humility to be authentic.

Growing up, we used to travel as a family to visit Daddy's parents, Mother and Daddy Graham, in Charlotte, North Carolina. To get there, we passed through a little town called Marion, home to Gibbs Steak House. Gibbs was famous in those parts for keeping black bears in a cage near the front of the restaurant. Stopping to eat there was always one of the highlights of our journey, and for us children, it might have been the pinnacle. We lived on a mountain with wildlife,

MY GRANDPARENTS, FRANK AND MORROW GRAHAM

but at Gibbs we got to watch — and smell — the bears up close and personal.

On one particular visit to Gibbs, after we had finished our meal and were headed outside to look at the bears, Daddy was told that another patron in the restaurant had covered our bill. He expressed surprise over this. Then someone in our group piped up, "I wish I had known — I would've gotten something more expensive!" Not at all happy with this remark, Daddy sternly replied: "Don't you say that! That was very nice of that person, and we are to be grateful. So many people in the world don't have anything at all."

My father's rebuke at Gibbs was nothing we hadn't heard before — he has never been one to take things for granted. He grew up the son of a farmer, milking cows twice a day on the dairy owned by his father and uncle, and usually began work at 2:30 in the morning. Daddy has noted that his mother was out picking beans on the day she gave birth to him; and, ultimately, I believe, he still sees himself through the lenses of these beginnings: as a farmer's kid reared by honorable, hardworking parents and in the company of good country folk.

Many times my father has wondered aloud why God would choose a farmer's kid to share the gospel on such a large scale. In his autobiography, he wrote, "I have often said that the first thing I am going to do when I get to Heaven is to ask, 'Why me, Lord? Why did You choose a farm boy from North Carolina to preach to so many people, to have such a wonderful team of associates, and to have a part in what You were doing in the latter half of the twentieth century?'"[1]

My father has never lost sight of where he came from; he understands the ministry only carries influence because God chose to give it influence. Nothing Daddy did earned him the destiny God gave him. He knows it, and his family knows it. In a 1970s interview, Mother Graham said of her son's impact on the world, "I don't think it's anything Billy has; I don't think it's anything that we can look back on from his childhood. I think the Lord has definitely picked Billy up and given him a gift in this age … I believe it's a real gift from God. There's no other answer in my own heart."

Daddy's lack of pretension shows up in small, everyday ways. In company, he always takes the first steps to introduce himself in order to put others at ease. He can converse with people of any estate and make them feel his equal. He dresses in whatever he happens to pull out of the closet: usually something like blue jeans, a threadbare jean shirt with a velour pullover, and, perhaps, bright-colored socks.

He puts a particularly high premium on manners. My father has spent a lifetime opening doors for women and standing when others enter his presence. Having become physically frail with age, he now apologizes for his inability to fulfill his responsibilities of courtesy — although, to him these "responsibilities" are not so much duties as sincere expressions of politeness and love. He wants others to feel valued.

DADDY AND T.W. WILSON
("UNCLE T") FISHING
WITH MY CHILDREN, 1982

## HUMILITY THROUGH WEAKNESS

Physical limitations are not new to my father; over decades of ministry, his body has come under incredible strain. Daddy wrote about the physical demands of his calling in his autobiography: "A doctor who was also an evangelist once told me that the hardest work a person can do is preach an evangelistic sermon. Whether that is true or not, I don't know. What I *do* know is that evangelistic preaching is physically and emotionally draining. One reason it is draining for me is that I am constantly driving for commitment. Another reason is that speaking of matters with eternal consequences is a great responsibility, and I am always afraid I won't make the message clear or will say something that is misleading.... Preaching also involves us in a spiritual battle with the forces of evil." [2]

Traveling around the world from crusade to crusade, Daddy battled illnesses, fevers, dramatic weight loss, and exhaustion as a matter of course. The Mayo Clinic was routinely his first stop after his meetings; it also took him time to recover strength once he finally got back to Montreat. My father communicated his ailments to us in detail so that we would keep him in prayer, but we often teased that perhaps he was really a hypochondriac. In her book *It's My Turn*, Mother explained Daddy's family nickname, "Puddleglum," taken from a C. S. Lewis character in the children's book *The Silver Chair*. Puddleglum tends to see the gloomy side of every situation, and our family lovingly jokes with Daddy about his tendency to do the same, especially concerning his health. When I had gallbladder surgery some years ago, Daddy, true to form, asked me to describe my symptoms, and as I described them, he began to wonder if he might have the same problem!

Whatever we might say in jest, my father's physical issues have been manifold and often unusual, some of them resulting from mishaps that occurred even at home. A ram, for instance, butted Daddy down a hillside in our pasture, causing him to tear a ligament in his knee. He also suffered a potentially fatal spider bite from a brown recluse. For days he complained to Mother about the red spot and swelling, but she thought he was being overly concerned. It wasn't until he got to Mayo's that he was diagnosed.

Daddy has had bouts with pneumonia; kidney stones; prostate cancer; thrombophlebitis; pseudomonas, a bacterial infection in his lungs; and hydrocephalus (fluid buildup on the brain), which imitates Parkinson's disease, causing trembling and lack of balance. Looking back, I can only imagine the strain these health battles must have caused my parents, though when we were growing up, Mother never seemed anxious when Daddy was ill. I followed Mother's example and tended not to worry, but I do remember being scared after my father had surgery once. Overhearing Uncle T tell the headmaster of my boarding school that Daddy had lost a lot of blood during the operation, I suddenly felt terrified — and, for the first time, aware of my father's mortality.

Daddy has said to me more than once that God has used his illnesses to keep him humble and dependent. Because he was so vulnerable to physical debilitation, he explained, he could never mistake what God did through him for something he had accomplished on his own. God simply had to do the work — and, therefore, it was God who got the credit. My father knew he was only an instrument; his weakness constantly reminded him. Here he is describing the back-breaking experience of preaching at the 1957 New York City meetings, a crusade originally scheduled for six weeks but spanning a marathon sixteen:

> *I had nothing to give. I had exhausted my material. I had exhausted my body. I had exhausted my mind. Yet the preaching had far more power. It was God taking sheer weakness — it is when I get out of the way and say, God, You have to do it. I sat on the platform many nights with nothing to say, nothing. Just sat there. And I knew that in a few minutes I'd have to get up and preach, and I'd just say, Oh, God, I can't do it! And yet, I would stand up and all of a sudden it would begin to come ... just God giving it, that's all.*[3]

DADDY IN MADISON
SQUARE GARDEN, 1957

## Total Dependence on God

One of the remarkable things about my father — the key to his ministry's influence, I believe — is this unyielding awareness that God is the one doing the real work. Obviously, my father worked hard, expending himself in ministry perhaps as much as a person can. He has said, for example, that he never fully bounced back physically from the 1957 New York meetings, never recovered what he poured out during those sixteen weeks of preaching. But while he has given everything in the effort of his calling, my father has always known that the ministry's real success — its success in touching lives — comes from God.

For example, at a 1973 crusade in Atlanta, Georgia, a man approached Daddy and began to praise him with great enthusiasm for his work. I stood by listening as my father warmly responded, saying, "I just happened to be in town when the Spirit was working."

Daddy was not being coy to the man who complimented him; he wasn't trying to *appear* humble. My father has never been casual about giving God the credit for the work of the ministry. He is very aware that God will not share his glory with another (Isaiah 42:8); and besides that, my father knows that God *must* do the work. Not only because Daddy himself is physically vulnerable, lacking the stamina to do what is required of him; but also because no mere man has the power to change the heart of another human being. The human heart is the province of God. God made the heart. A man is just a man.

"I am always deeply conscious," Daddy wrote in his autobiography, "that I am absolutely helpless and that only the Holy Spirit can penetrate the minds and hearts of those who are without Christ. When I am speaking from the Bible, I know there is also another voice speaking to the people, and that is the voice of the Holy Spirit. I am reminded often of Jesus' parable of the seed and the sower… knowing that all I am doing is sowing seed. It is God — and only God — who can make that seed bear fruit." [4]

Found in this explanation, I believe, are the truths that have driven my father at the most fundamental level. Simply put, he understands *his* part in the ministry — "speaking from the Bible;" and he understands *God's* part — "to penetrate the minds and hearts" of those who hear. Aware of the difference, and keenly aware of his need for God's help even in doing his own small part, my father has practiced a level of dependence on God that can only be the fruit of real humility.

On the platform, Daddy has depended on God to strengthen him, to speak through him, and then to open the hearts of those listening. Off the platform, he has depended on God for every nut and bolt in the huge machinery of the ministry: for favor with other orga-

nizations and people of influence; for guidance concerning media interviews and publicity; for the strength of interpersonal relationships within his organization; for vindication and direction in the face of opposition from others; and for absolutely anything else pertaining to life and ministry that I could name. My father has lived out nothing short of total dependence on God. And from my earliest years, I saw that dependence in action. I couldn't help but see it. Everything from my father's casual conversation to the advice he gave regarding my smallest concerns conveyed dependence on God as the only way to live.

In a typical passage from a letter to my siblings and me during my school days, Daddy wrote: "The Apostle Paul said: 'I can do all things through Christ which strengtheneth me.' Bunny and Franklin, that means in your studies. If you will work hard and then turn the rest over to the Lord, He will help you." Later, Daddy gave me virtually the same advice — work hard and trust God — about communicating the gospel: "When it comes to the Gospel," he wrote, "—you be faithful and the Holy Spirit will do the communicating in a way you could never do."

Considering my father's genuine humility before God and his choice to lean on God for absolutely everything, this simple advice, adapted for my ever changing needs and concerns, seems the most authentic expression of my father's heart as any I can remember. It is the same wisdom he applied as he parented us, doing the best he could and leaving us in God's hands. It is the same wisdom he has given me since my childhood. *Do your part and God will do his part. Work hard and turn the rest over to God. Be faithful and the Holy Spirit will help you. Be married to Christ first and let him meet your needs.*

## DEPENDENCE ON GOD THROUGH PRAYER

One recent morning, I was sitting with my father in his bedroom while he ate breakfast. He sat in a tall chair, meant to decrease stress on his hips, and he talked with my grandson and me while he sipped his coffee.

As we chatted about current events, I found myself preoccupied with some things my father had shared the previous evening after dinner. Sitting at the table that evening, I had asked him questions about his work, hoping to glean wisdom about how to approach some opportunities in my own life. I had wanted to talk to my father for some time.

He began by reflecting on his engagements at Oxford and Cambridge Universities in 1955 and 1980, noting how much he had enjoyed the Q-&-A exchanges with the college students. He had also visited Ivy League schools in New England in 1982 and engaged those students in a similar fashion.

"Did you ever feel intimidated?" I asked, referring to the intellectual prowess of his listeners.

"Not at all," he replied.

When I asked him how he prepared for his engagements in light of the incredible demands on his attention and the diversity of his audiences, he replied, simply, "I prayed."

Now, the morning after this dinner conversation, sitting with my father in his room while he ate breakfast, I wanted to go deeper. After he pointed out some things in the room to my young grandson, I went back to the subject of the night before.

"Daddy," I asked, perhaps knowing the answer, but needing him to share more with me, "did you ever feel inadequate?"

"All the time," he replied.

"You said that to get prepared for your engagements you prayed. But *how* did you pray?"

He said that he prepared for ministry by asking the Holy Spirit to help him. He asked for help in everything he faced. Sometimes, he explained, "help me" was all he could pray. He told me that whenever he was back at home with us in Montreat preparing for his meetings, specifically before London 1954 and New York 1957, he would sit in a rocking chair on the front porch at Chapman Home, a lodge on a nearby mountain, and pray for hours at a time.

Growing up, I don't recall running into my father while he was praying privately, but I certainly knew he prayed a lot. Prayer was part of his daily conversation — he never made any significant decisions without consulting the Lord. He talked about praying; he asked us to pray for him; he urged us to pray with him. "Let's pray about this," he would say. Or: "Have you prayed about that?" Or: "Please pray for our team. Pray for our upcoming meetings. Pray for my strength." And, of course, when he was at home, he led our family in prayer. Mornings and evenings every day we had family devotions, kneeling to pray, and Daddy would lead.

One special time of prayer with my father stands out. I had been a student at boarding school in Florida for a couple of years, and now Mother and Daddy wanted to enroll me in the school in New York. I hated the thought of leaving my friends in Florida and starting over at another school; I didn't want to make the change. One morning when I was back at home, Daddy called Mother and me into his room, explaining that the three of us needed to pray for God's direction about my schooling. We all knelt by my father's bed, and he led us in prayer.

Immediately, it became clear to me that I needed to consent to what my parents wanted for me. I needed to obey their wishes and quit resisting. Our time together in prayer sealed my understanding of the change being required of me. Trusting God, I realized, meant trusting my parents. In retrospect, I see that by calling me to pray with him and Mother about the decision, Daddy was teaching me something vital about humility. For in agreeing to pray for, and submit to, God's direction, I was learning the posture of the humble heart as expressed by Jesus when he prayed, "not my will, but Yours be done" (Luke 22:42 NASB).

Getting up from my father's bedside, I agreed — albeit sorrowfully — to go to New York.

## THE POSTURE OF THE LEARNER

I have always known my father to operate out of an intense desire to improve himself — whether by staying current with news, reading books on various subjects, or absorbing wisdom from others. He is extremely curious and is constantly asking questions. Ever aware of his need for growth, he maintains the posture of a learner — which is a posture of humility.

Now in his late eighties, my father spends hours each day reading, usually propped up in his bed, which is framed on each side by bookcases — in fact, the room's paneled walls are lined with bookcases. He subscribes to an array of magazines and newspapers, including the *Charlotte Observer*, *Asheville Citizen-Times*, *New York Times,* and *The Times of London*. When he was still preaching, he would subscribe to the publications that corresponded with his event schedule. In early 2005, for example, he took an additional number of New York papers to prepare for his final crusade, scheduled for late June in New York City.

My father doesn't read with a lot of props like notebooks and highlighters. He just takes notes, usually with felt-tip pens, in the book or Bible he happens to be reading. I have a Bible that contains his handwritten sermon notes in the margins and an outline inside the front cover.

Because he loves to read, I usually give my father books for Christmas. One year I gave him a biography of George Washington that he referenced several times during dinner conversation. Following the September 11th attacks, he did extensive reading on Islam and its history, often raising the subject for discussion when I visited him. He becomes particularly energized during stimulating talk.

In some way, I believe my father's drive to learn and expand himself partly informed his decision when I was young to take me out of my Florida boarding school — a familiar, social, evangelical environment — and enroll me in the New York boarding school where I struggled to adapt. The New York school was known for its academic reputation. Its religious bent was Episcopalian, which at that time was unfamiliar to me. In the cold climate and somewhat alien cultural and religious environment of the school, I felt like a fish out of water. But my father would not take me out. Both he and my mother recognized the challenges were forcing me to grow and mature as both a young woman and a Christian. Exposed to people different from myself, I was growing in an awareness of the world, and this was what my parents wanted: they were determined that my perspective and knowledge base be continually expanding, even as they were working to enlarge their own.

## LEARNING FOR THE GOSPEL'S SAKE

Like so much else in his life, my father's desire to learn ultimately stems from his desire to "do his part" and be the best he can be for God and the work of the ministry. Beyond his natural curiosity, Daddy pursues learning in order to become a better communicator of the gospel. He has always sought to engage a wide variety of people — people of different faiths, cultural backgrounds, and theological perspectives — in an effort to broaden his understanding of issues in society and the world. While never compromising the gospel message, Daddy is not wed to his own way of thinking. He enters into dialogue with an open heart and an eagerness to listen. He wants to be informed.

Among his friends, my father has counted a spectrum of leaders and thinkers, from major American interfaith leader Rabbi Marc Tanenbaum to Swiss-German theologian Karl Barth. I remember Daddy meeting with Dr. Barth in the summer of 1960. Our family had been loaned a house in Switzerland while my father held crusades in Europe, and we went as a family to visit the Barth home. Then nine years old, I played with Dr. Barth's grandchildren, and I recall seeing him walk down the hillside with Daddy after their meeting had concluded.

TOGETHER IN SWITZERLAND, SUMMER 1960

My father's call for World Congresses on Evangelism, beginning in the 1960s, was partly an outgrowth of his determination to learn and grow. He wanted to know what was happening around the world in the area of evangelistic outreach, and through the congresses, he sought to find out how he could support and enhance those efforts on a global scale. He and his team planned the congresses with a vision to rally the worldwide church to its call of evangelism, but my father attended the congresses — and addressed them — as a learner.

He set such an example for me in this that when I attended the second congress, this one in Lausanne, Switzerland, in 1974, I attempted to read as many of the plenary addresses beforehand as I could to stay abreast of the issues. I knew these meetings were important to Daddy, so I tried in a feeble way to understand the content. In fact, it was here at these meetings that I first felt a stirring to reach out beyond myself and serve God in a broader capacity — a desire that would not be fulfilled until much later. I was determined to learn as much as possible from the historic experience and come away better equipped to share God's Word in my sphere of influence, and I am sure this passionate resolve was largely instilled in me by my father.

Throughout his years in ministry, Daddy has sought with particular passion to understand the issues preoccupying the hearts and minds of young people, the world's future leaders, in order to communicate the gospel to them in relevant ways. My father has described the strong burden he felt for "the rootlessness of the sixties generation" — one that came of age amid tremendous unrest — and he wrote a book called *The Jesus Generation* for those, including myself, who belonged to that group.[5]

More recently, I witnessed a powerful instance of my father's effort to connect with youth when I attended his 1994 meetings in Atlanta, Georgia. At the beginning of the Saturday evening service, designated as youth night and called "Jammin' in the Dome," the arena boomed with the heavy beats of Christian rock music. Some of the older people complained it was too loud — not conducive to a worship service. And from where I stood, I could see expressions of disapproval on their faces. But the music was geared toward the youth — it was their night — and they made up most of the thousands in the audience.

After the rock music ended, recording artist Michael W. Smith came out and quieted the crowd with a peaceful song. In the now hushed and dim stadium, my father, dressed in shirt sleeves, walked across the platform and sat down cross-legged on the floor.

All movement ceased, and I listened as my father, then seventy-five years old, talked directly to the young people, who had come from the stands to gather in front of the platform. Daddy was face-to-face with them. He spoke quietly — not as a zealous preacher, but as a loving, patient grandfather. He addressed the issues the youth were facing and talked to them about finding meaning in life, drawing from John 3:16, "For God so loved the world …" The packed arena was so still you could hear a pin drop, and it struck me that Daddy was making an impact on the youth with the gospel, not only because he had reached out to them culturally through music; but also because he was willing to relate to them at their level, willing to understand, willing to listen, willing to learn. His love, his humility — these were what drew his young audience to him.

## STUDENT OF THE WORLD

On a larger scale, my father has applied the same "learner's approach" to ministry while traveling the world speaking to people of diverse backgrounds. In this way, his humility has informed the very heart of his work in mass evangelism. To prepare for his meetings, for example, my father would study and consult with experts in an effort to understand the cultures of the people to whom he would speak — their ways of thinking and seeing the world; the ways they expressed deeply held beliefs; the obstacles to the message of the gospel embedded within cultures; and the opportunities those cultures afforded the gospel. As was his approach with the youth of America, Daddy sought to meet people where they were. He went to them, physically and in every way he possibly could. He humbled and extended himself, adapting his methods and vocabulary. And he brought with him a burning desire to touch hearts with the message of Christ in a way that could be understood, and, ultimately, embraced.

I had the opportunity to study my father's approach to cross-cultural communications in ministry during the years I spent completing my undergraduate degree at Mary Baldwin College. Majoring in religion and communications, I decided to write my thesis on Daddy's two-and-a-half-week trip to China in 1988 and examine the ways he presented the gospel message — particularly the biblical concepts of God, sin, and salvation — in the context of Chinese culture.

To say the experience was an eye-opener would be an understatement. I came to the project somewhat naïve. I thought it would be easy. I was close to the material, and I was passionate about it — not just about the ministry, but also about my father's trip to China, where Mother grew up. I had listened to stories of the Chinese people all my life from both my mother and my grandparents, who were medical missionaries. Mother's tastes and her way of seeing the world reflected Chinese culture. China was a part of her, and she was a part of China. For us, my father's first trip to Mother's native land was deeply personal.

Having heard so much about the 1988 China trip, having been aware — or so I thought — of the preparations involved, I assumed that writing my undergraduate thesis would be a straightforward process. I was mistaken. Pursuing a detailed understanding of my father's approach to ministry, I found, was like trying to wrap my arms around a hot air balloon! I discovered that knowing Daddy as a person and studying him as a man with a task of historical significance were two different things entirely.

## HUMILITY IN CHINA

Chinese culture is a difficult one to "bridge" for an American Christian evangelist. Beyond the general resistance to foreign ideas in China — and to religious faiths considered foreign — there are few ready concepts within the culture to which one can relate the gospel. In preparing for his trip, my father first had to locate a vocabulary the Chinese could understand as he communicated the message of Christ.

Daddy began by creating a team of consultants with wide-ranging expertise on China and did a great deal of personal reading and research. Mother, who was intimately involved in the preparations, vigorously coached Daddy on the nuances of the culture. My father was looking for general areas of need within Chinese culture

DADDY AT THE GREAT WALL OF CHINA, 1988

that the Christian message could fulfill. In the end, he decided to emphasize issues of peace, spiritual hunger, patriotism as an outgrowth of the Christian life, and his own personal faith in Christ.

To successfully communicate in these areas, Daddy had to work around the fact that none of the major Chinese religions included the concept of a loving, personal God. He constructed one of his sermons, for instance, around the question, "Is there a God and can he be known?" Also, in a culture lacking the familiar Western understanding of original sin, Daddy had to find a way to help his listeners grasp the basis of their need for God. Since Chinese culture is relational, my father emphasized sin as a breaking of relationship with God and salvation as a restoring of that relationship.

My father's talks were rich with illustrations from everyday life experiences — like farming, banquets, and immunizations — and laced with quotes from Confucius, Einstein, Pascal, Dostoyevsky, and the Bible. He also shared personal details about his own spiritual journey, referencing his farming background as a means of connection. "I was born and reared in the southern part of the United States," he explained, "and my boyhood years were spent on my parents' small farm. But one day I came to the realization that something was wrong inside me . . .

that there was an emptiness in my heart that nothing could fill and a yearning for meaning and purpose in life. The time came when I made a personal commitment to Christ."[6]

What I discovered researching my thesis and digging into the ministry's inner workings was that my father was successful in China because he approached the culture with humility. He went to China asking questions and emphasizing areas of common interest. He demonstrated respect for the Chinese people and a sincere desire to learn from them. Everywhere he went he graciously shared his appreciation of China's history and culture. And, ultimately, because he was flexible, interested, and sensitive, he was able to communicate the gospel as a universal message — not a Western idea; and one that the Chinese could embrace while remaining themselves.

MOTHER AND DADDY WITH CHINESE PREMIER LI PENG, 1988

## Ultimate Example

My deep study of the China trip and what it required of my father changed my view of his work — I felt like a curtain had been drawn aside allowing me to see the whole production. I considered the creativity and innovation my father mustered to connect with the Chinese; the energy he brought to the task; the sense of purpose driving him; the love that informed his words, actions, and attitude. Then I reflected on the tightrope he had to walk as a communicator and the care with which he had to speak to avoid causing offense. With the help of an extraordinary and committed team, Daddy managed to cover his bases. He was able to study and absorb the material so that it became a part of him. He then communicated to the Chinese in a way that was natural and authentic, carrying his message with conviction, yet delivering it with care.

Of course, I realized that the only way my father had been able to keep a thousand plates spinning and still connect with the hearts of his listeners went back to the fundamental way he lives his life. Here was a situation — if ever there was one — that required my father to work hard and turn the rest over to the Lord. In China Daddy had to depend on God for every word he spoke, for every interaction with officials, and for favor with the government to accomplish the things he believed God wanted him to do. He had to be careful too not to say anything that would discredit Chinese Christians. Had my father not known how to trust God in that setting, he might have crumbled under the pressure. In many ways, the China trip was, for me, the ultimate example of my father's humility before God.

And the China trip was only one of countless such trips my father made, traveling to every continent in the world. I had studied only two-and-a-half weeks in what is now a career spanning some six decades! Writing my thesis helped me register just how big the ministry was, and is — so much bigger than my father or mother, than our family, than the BGEA team, than my experience of the crusades. I was overwhelmed by the enormity of the work and the sovereignty of God in choosing my father to lead it. In no way was the ministry about my father. What God had accomplished through him was just that — what *God* had accomplished *through* him.

In light of this understanding, I learned to better appreciate my father and his sacrifices; and I realized my own sacrifice in letting him go for the ministry was small compared with God's plan to touch the world through a humble farmer's kid from North Carolina. I am so proud of Daddy, and I am humbled to have been chosen to be his child. I only pray that I can live a life half as submitted to the plans and purposes of God. My journey and purpose are different from my father's, but from his example I see that no matter my calling, trusting and depending on God are the keys to making an impact for Christ on the world around me.

- CHAPTER FOUR -

*Grace*

*For of His fullness we have all received, and grace upon grace.*

JOHN 1:16 NASB

I stood in the doorframe of the kitchen and faced my parents, who were drinking coffee and sitting in the two overstuffed armchairs in front of the bay window. A fire burned in the big stone fireplace. Through the window I could see the valley, its trees stripped bare, and the mountains in the distance. It was February.

"Can I read you something?" I asked.

I had been home for a couple of weeks. I had driven to Montreat with my fifteen-year-old daughter, now returned to boarding school, and my most valuable possessions in the back of my station wagon. I left my house in Florida in a hurry — in flight from a second marriage that had broken down leaving me fearful for my personal safety and overwhelmed with shame for the mistake I had made in going through with the marriage in the first place. It had been a few years since my first marriage ended in divorce. Family members had warned me about entering marriage again so soon, but I had not listened. Stubborn and willful, I believed I was the better judge. Now, devastated, I saw just how wrong my judgment had been. The second marriage had collapsed in a matter of weeks.

"I have a letter here," I said to Mother and Daddy, holding up the sheets of paper. I was using the time in Montreat to stabilize, and I had prepared a letter to my then-husband. I wanted to read it to my parents so they could offer input. I was depending on them now — I certainly didn't trust myself.

Mother smiled and motioned toward the kitchen table. I pulled out one of the chairs, sat down, and began to read.

My parents listened attentively as I struggled through the letter, stifling tears. I was thinking about the damage I had caused my children and the shame I had brought on my family. Mother and Daddy were eager to help in any way they could, but I wondered what they must think of me. What a mess I had made! And here it was in black-and-white. I was spelling it out for them, all of the ugliness. What would they say?

Once I finished, I folded the letter and looked up. Daddy was gazing tenderly at me, his coffee mug resting in his lap. Too ashamed to meet his eye, I looked down at the letter again and braced myself for whatever was coming. I noticed my hands starting to shake.

Then my father spoke. He told me first that I had assumed an enormous amount of responsibility for what had happened in the conflict. After that he said something I will never forget.

"Ruth," he said gently, "don't be so hard on yourself. We all live under grace and do the best we can."

## Welcome Home

It took me a moment to register what my father had said. His words were so kind, so loving. Even as he was talking about grace, he was demonstrating it. I suppose I shouldn't have been surprised. Daddy had been kind to me since the day I arrived home from Florida — literally, since the moment I arrived.

I thought back to that moment now. Driving up my parents' driveway with my daughter, herself confused and upset, was one of the hardest things I had ever done. Completely exhausted, I simply had no idea what to expect from my parents, and I feared the worst. Here I had gone and remarried against the urgent advice of loved ones. Now I was basically on the run with my daughter and a car full of valuables. What would Mother and Daddy say? Would they reject me? Would they dismiss me as having "made my bed" and tell me to lie in it?

What followed was one of the defining moments in my life. As I rounded the bend at the top of the driveway, I saw my father standing near the front of the house. Stopping the car, I tried to prepare to face him. I turned off the ignition and opened the door. I took a deep breath. Then, stifling my emotion, I got out of the car. And as I did, my father, who had every right to be ashamed of me, wrapped his arms around me and said, "Welcome home."

At home with Daddy, 1993

I have written at length about my father's embrace at that moment. His total acceptance of me in one of the darkest periods of my life changed me. Standing there in front of him, I felt worthless, a failure. How could anyone, least of all my father, welcome me? I felt I had disappointed and embarrassed him — big time.

Yet he demonstrated unconditional love. In wrapping his arms around me as we stood beside my car, my father showed me the heavenly Father's love, forgiveness, and grace. Like the father in the biblical story of the prodigal son — the father who stood in the road watching for his son's return from a life of sin and ruin; the father who, when he saw his son coming, ran out to meet him — like *this* father, my own father had come to my side to embrace me. He left no room for me to fear his condemnation; he silenced that fear with love before I could even look into his face.

But standing in the kitchen reading my parents the letter to my husband seemed a different matter. By then I had been home for weeks. I was broken, but not nearly as fragile as when Daddy had first greeted me in the driveway. The pain over my situation was deep but not quite as raw. My father could have taken the opportunity to be stern. He could have pointed out my mistakes. He could have blamed me for the ordeal. I had invited him to give his input, after all. But Daddy responded just as he had that first day when I arrived — he responded with grace. Seeing that I was trying to take responsibility for my actions, he extended his "Welcome home" beyond our greeting in the driveway and dealt with me gently as I tried to pick up the pieces of my life.

## LIVING UNDER GRACE

What did my father mean by his statement, "We all live under grace and do the best we can"? What does it mean to "live under grace"?

Grace might be described as the undeserved kindness of God. Flawed as we are, God extends grace — kindness, acceptance, welcome — to us through Jesus Christ. When we invite Christ into our lives and decide to follow him, God gives us a new, clean heart. He forgives our sin and changes us so that we can live in friendship with him. This kind of grace some have called "saving grace."

But we also need grace for everyday living, or, "living grace." We all make mistakes. We make wrong choices, as I did when I entered that second marriage. We sin. We mess up our lives. And when we do, God is there to help us. He provides grace, or help, in times of need (Hebrews 4:16). He gives us grace, or strength, in our weakness (2 Corinthians 12:9). He offers grace, or forgiveness, when we sin (Ephesians 1:7).

We are so used to having strings attached to gifts that it is difficult to imagine God's grace is free and abundant. One of my favorite Bible verses is, "For of His fullness we have all received, and grace upon grace" (John 1:16 NASB). While we can't just go out and do as we please expecting God to forgive us, presuming on his grace, in our deepest failures and moral crises, grace is available. When my father said, "We all live under grace," he was being a channel of God's kindness to me. He was saying, in effect: *It's all right. God still loves you. He will turn this mess into something useful. Don't allow your failure and sin to crush you. Trust God. His grace is sufficient for you — even now.*

Daddy wasn't glossing over my sin or ignoring the depth of the damage I had caused myself and others. He grieved over the pain and heartache. He was distressed over what I had done. He knew my willfulness in going forward with the marriage was wrong. But he also knew my own grief. Since my arrival I had spent hours pouring out my heart to my parents. By the time I read my parents the letter in the kitchen, my father knew I was trying to follow God. He knew how responsible I felt, how hard I was taking my failure, and how badly I wanted to do my part to change.

As I sat there at the table, tears running down my face and the letter I had just read shaking in my hands, Daddy knew I had done the necessary spiritual "plowing" of repentance in my own heart.

Now, by his kind words, he was "planting" the seeds of grace.

## DOING THE BEST WE CAN

My father's words made a life-giving impact on me at a critical time. Over the years, I have shared his words with other hurting people, explaining that as we repent of our sin, doing the best we can, God is faithful to help us. In this respect, the grace my father both spoke about and offered to me that February when I hit bottom is part of his legacy — one that is giving life to people he will never know.

But even beyond his words, beyond important displays of acceptance like his "Welcome home," my father has consistently modeled what it means to live under grace and do the best he can. Really, I am back to the advice he has given me on so many different occasions: *Do your part and God will do his part. Work hard and turn the rest over to God. Be faithful and the Holy Spirit will do what only he can do.* I could easily add to this list, *Live under grace and do the best you can.* In each of Daddy's statements the components are the same: God has a part to play. And so do we.

No matter how often I reflect on my father's life and ministry, I am always struck by his ability to live in the balance between the two pieces of his advice — trusting God on the one hand and working hard on the other. Daddy knows how to depend on God's grace. He has always understood that his own small efforts were not enough to carry him in preaching the gospel to the nations, making relationships work, handling opposition, enduring temptation, and being a loving husband and father. As I have shared, my father has lived a life of dependence on God, looking to him to do what only he, the Lord, can do.

But, as I have also shared, my father does his part. He does what only *he* can do. He does his best, which involves obedience to God — obedience not just in the big things, like taking the gospel around the world; but in private matters too, like being accountable in personal financial dealings, for example. In her book, *It's My Turn*, Mother wrote: "Bill is highly disciplined and drives himself unmercifully."[1] My father is not perfect; I'm sure there have been occasions when he felt he did not do his best. But those of us who know him would say such instances are exceptions. Whether Daddy *feels* he has done his best, we recognize, in my mother's words, that my father is a man who "drives himself unmercifully."

Doing one's best, I believe, is really an issue of character. Even as I write — setting down observations, illustrations, and thoughts about my father — I am becoming more impressed with the depth of his character. Character comes with a price. To develop character, we must learn how to get up and try again when we fall; we must face moral dilemmas and learn how to make right decisions; we must see our commitment tested in various contexts; we must persevere through challenges. We are not born with character — we build it. Since I have known him, my father has worked doggedly to develop a character pleasing to God. He is determined to obey God and do his best, and he never lets up. He keeps the end in view, desiring with all his heart to hear God say, "Well done, good and faithful servant" (Matthew 25:23 KJV).

## DOING HIS BEST THROUGH DISCIPLINE

A familiar scene in my memory is that of my father — wearing jeans, a thick, worn suede jacket, and a golf cap — walking up and down our steep driveway in Montreat, accompanied by a German shepherd, and my mother, who trails them both in a golf cart.

Daddy is in his seventies in this scene. By this time Mother is suffering the effects of degenerative arthritis, but she is determined to get out on her beloved property, smell the air, look at the trees, and note changes to the land, keeping an eye out for things that need tending.

Coming down from the house, the three take a sharp curve to the right, and then reach an area of the driveway that levels off for about a tenth of a mile. Sloping down on one side of the drive is the gully pasture — the one where Daddy was butted down the hillside by an

ornery ram; and beyond the pasture, a wood of tall hardwood trees and poplars extending to the top of the ridge farther off. On the other side of the driveway, a steep embankment teems with daffodils and rhododendron bushes — one bush for each grandchild.

When they reach this section of the driveway, Daddy and his dog might jog the level stretch of pavement back and forth for a mile or two. Mother might follow along in her golf cart for some of these "laps," chatting with Daddy about ideas for improving the property. (As Daddy aged, she ordered benches to be placed at short intervals along the driveway so that he could sit and rest.) Eventually, once my parents are refreshed, they will make their way back up to the house.

I have watched my father practice the discipline of physical activity since I can remember. When I was a little girl, Daddy would spend hours out on the mountain hiking or jogging, and this was before jogging was popular. He frequently played golf, his favorite form of exercise. During crusades he would try to jog most days; and during trips to the beach for vacation, he took numerous long walks along the shore. More recently, family friends had a small lap pool built behind our house, where my father still swims as part of his physical therapy.

During long trips, my father understood that if he did not maintain a certain level of physical fitness, he would never be able to stand on a platform preaching every night as weeks turned into months. Of course, even when Daddy was in good physical condition, the hard-driving pace took its toll and he succumbed to illness, which meant that if he didn't do his best to get ready for the stress of a crusade, he could end up in very bad shape. My father counted on the grace of God to get him through his exhaustion, but he did not take that grace for granted.

## STUDY TO SHOW YOURSELF APPROVED

If there is an area in which my father has consistently done his best, it is in preparation for preaching. For some six decades of ministry, he has given his all to studying for his sermons. He understands that the grace of God needs a prepared mind on which to operate. How, as the Scripture says, can the Holy Spirit bring God's Word to my father's memory for preaching if there is not enough material in his mind to start with? (John 14:26)

When I was growing up, my father spent hours at his desk, immersing himself in the Scriptures and other readings to prepare for his meetings. He normally kept a Dictaphone on one side of his desk and files on the other, along with a large photograph of Mother. Atop a mass of papers and books would lay an open Bible. Bookshelves lined the walls of his study, and while he worked, he could look out on the courtyard from a large picture window flanked by two comfortable armchairs.

My father read all that he could on relevant subjects — the works

of people like John Stott, James Montgomery Boice, and other Bible scholars and theologians. Further influences — both literary and hands-on — were Carl Henry, the first editor of *Christianity Today*, which Daddy co-founded with my grandfather; Harold Lindsell, *Christianity Today*'s second editor; Donald Grey Barnhouse, whose periodical, *Eternity*, made a particular impact on my father; V. Raymond Edman, former president of Wheaton College; Robert Evans, founder of Greater Europe Mission; and my mother's father, Nelson Bell — retired missionary, esteemed surgeon, one-time moderator of the Southern Presbyterian Church, and executive editor and co-founder of *Christianity Today*. Daddy spoke to my grandfather almost daily, and my grandfather's fingerprints are all over both my father and the ministry.

My father always said that preparing his messages required tremendous focus and energy. He did use researchers and writers, and Mother kept files of illustrations from her own reading; she was an invaluable help. But the bulk of the work and responsibility, of course, was on Daddy. His messages in the end had to be those God had given to him to preach. He took nothing for granted. He never just rehashed an old message. He might have used old material, but he reworked it to make it relevant to his listeners. Not long ago he was feeling the pressure of some upcoming meetings, and my mother encouraged him to "pull out an old message." He said to me later, "I just can't do that. I have to make the message fresh."

In his autobiography, my father explained his approach: "Ruth [my mother] maintained in her counsel and advice to me that my studies should consist primarily of filling up spiritually; she believed, as I did, that God would give me the message and bring to remembrance in my preaching the things I had studied. This was always the most effective preaching, we had discovered: preaching that came from the overflow of a heart and mind filled not only with the Spirit but with much reading. Hence, I picked each sermon topic carefully, read myself full, wrote myself empty, and read myself full again on the subject."[2]

Daddy prepared most of his messages in advance of his meetings — crusade schedules could be frenzied, including press conferences, civic luncheons, and meetings with dignitaries. Nonetheless, even on site at a crusade, my father maintained his discipline of study. A case of books accompanied him wherever he traveled so that he could have access to his resource materials, and at some of his meetings, when the team saw they were going to have to extend the schedule to meet the interest and response in a given city, Daddy would have to study whenever he could in order to produce new messages. During his famous London campaign of 1954 — an intensive series of meetings that ended up lasting three months — some fifty of Daddy's seventy-two major evening messages had to be prepared the day they were preached.

AT HOME IN HIS STUDY, 1965

And yet, because my father maintained a lifestyle of study, when ministry required him to turn out his messages literally overnight, he did not have to pull material out of thin air. He could build on the foundation of material he had been studying all along. God could use my father in unexpected ways, bringing to Daddy's mind countless examples and truths from the Scriptures, because my father had done his part to get ready. He had not presumed on God's grace. He had obeyed what Paul commanded Timothy: "Be diligent to present yourself" — or, echoing the King James Version, study to show yourself — "approved to God as a workman who does not need to be ashamed, accurately handling the word of truth" (2 Timothy 2:15 NASB).

## JOY IN DISCIPLINE

In a way, I have difficulty associating the idea of "discipline" with my father's passion to study the Bible. When I think of discipline, what comes to mind is forcing myself to do something I don't feel inclined to do. Unlike my father, for instance, I struggle to stick to a regular exercise routine — I just don't like to exercise. I would much rather watch the morning news, have another cup of coffee, or go out to lunch with a friend. But I know that in order to stay healthy, maintain strength, and release stress, I must exercise. Even though I don't like it, I knuckle down and discipline myself to do it.

But no one has ever had to twist Daddy's arm to study the Bible. Studying for him is not just an act of obedience; it's not just about discipline or doing his best. My father loves the Scriptures. Last year when he was recovering in the hospital from a broken pelvis, he took out a new translation of the Bible and began reading just for the pure pleasure of it. Free from the pressure to extract sermon material, he didn't mark in the Bible or take any notes. He simply read the Scriptures in order to absorb them. This was the way he chose to spend his recovery.

Far from a mere "discipline," Daddy's study of the Scriptures seems to invigorate him. In 1976, he and Mother were staying with another couple on Mexico's Pacific coast, and in a letter to his board and family my father described the "penetrating power of the Word of God." He averaged four to five hours daily working on his book about the Holy Spirit during the trip, which I assume was designated as a time of rest; but that is just it — for my father, his work on the book was not "work." "This has been a time of more than disciplined study and writing," he wrote, "— it has been a time in which the Holy Spirit has used the study of 'Himself' to stir my own heart to a renewed commitment and surrender."

## TEACHING ME DISCIPLINE IN STUDY

Study of the Scriptures has always been Daddy's prescription for me too. As a young woman, newly married, I began to receive invitations to speak in various public forums. I was not yet twenty, but perhaps those who invited me believed that by virtue of my relationship with Daddy I would have wisdom to share. My father cautioned me very strongly against accepting such invitations. Addressing the issue by correspondence, he proposed a different course of action:

> *Bunny ... I personally would hate to see you get caught up in too much public speaking at your age. You could so easily be exploited in a way that would make it difficult to mature and develop normally. <u>You need study!</u> I long to see both you and Ted [my then-husband] go to Bible School — even taking evening classes.... But you could study <u>alone</u> and <u>together</u> if you are willing to discipline yourself ... or with Ted — or with a friend.... Take a book like Colossians — get Barclay's Commentary — and <u>study</u> and <u>study</u> till the book is "<u>yours</u>."*

My father was suggesting that study of the Scriptures would add substance and maturity to my character. I needed my own experience of the "penetrating power" of God's Word. I would not be able to minister to others just on the basis of my father's name — as Daddy implied, that scenario could be damaging. Knowing my vulnerability, he directed me to dig into the Scriptures myself, and in so directing

me, he gave me another glimpse of his own approach to study — one that is persistent, passionate, expectant, and, to use his own word, disciplined; which clearly, for him, did not reflect distaste. "Study till the book is '<u>yours</u>,'" he wrote. And in those words I saw his fervency for the Word of God and his trust in its authority.

Throughout their lives, both of my parents have shared their passion for the Scriptures with my siblings and me. They have shown us how to study the Bible — how to draw truths out of the Word of God and apply those truths to our lives. But they have also taught us to love the Bible and, more, to love the God of the Bible. The more we read about God, they taught us, the better we would know him. And the better we knew him, the more we would love him. And the more we loved him, the more we would trust him. Staying in the Scriptures would teach us one part of Daddy's advice — trusting God — even while we were doing the other part — working hard.

It does take discipline for me to study. Like my parents, I love the Scriptures, but there are days when studying is difficult, especially when I am preparing to teach. I don't always "feel" like doing it. The material may seem dry. There may be distractions. Yet because I have made the commitment to study, I sit down to honor that commitment and do my best. I read in the Scriptures until something speaks to me. I keep lists of God's attributes nearby in order to redirect my focus toward him if I see I'm getting off track. As I do these things, I find that God steps in and meets me with his grace. Eventually, pleasure comes. I may discover a new truth. I may find myself, having started in one subject, ending up in another subject altogether. Following cross-references becomes like following a trail. Study becomes an adventure!

My father must have had these kinds of experiences during the hours he spent preparing for ministry. "Live under grace and do the best you can" must not have been a principle that applied just to Daddy's work on a global level, but to his daily life, in the intimacy of his study or during his jogs on our mountain. Perhaps not feeling like giving his all, he simply sat down at his desk, or put on his jogging shoes, willing and present, and prayed for the grace to do his best, using those simple words: "Lord, help."

DADDY AND ME OUTSIDE MY HOME IN TEXAS, 1982

It must be my father's personal experience of God's kindness toward him over a lifetime that makes him so gracious to others. To me, it seems, Daddy has become even more grace-filled with age. In these later years, there is a gentleness about him that is so winsome. Our longtime family pastor, Calvin Thielman, once said, "The older you get, the more like yourself you become." My father is a gentle and gracious man and has become more so over the years.

Considering my father's mellowness, I think I have been more "warmed by the embers than by the fire." Of course, I greatly loved my father in his younger years, but something about the depth of his perspective as he has aged attracts me. My father stays true to the gospel without having a hard edge. He is not judgmental. He is not sharp-tongued. His life and ministry have been marked by an inclusiveness and love that only seem to expand.

Rarely — if ever — have I heard my father say a negative word about anyone. At times when I become critical of others, Daddy corrects me. "We don't know their heart or motives," he will caution. "We don't know what they were thinking." Or he might raise his eyebrows and say, "You don't know enough to make that assessment." Or he might communicate through silence, which can be the hardest response to bear.

But even when corrected, I appreciate my father's way of seeing the world — one that includes giving others the benefit of the doubt; one that does not presume to know the hearts of others. His perspective is Christlike. He sees with the eyes of grace.

I remember a recent conversation with my parents at the kitchen table in Montreat (so many of our significant moments seem to take place in that kitchen). I was asking Mother how to accept a child when you don't agree with him or her. I wanted to know how Mother had learned to find this kind of balance in her relationships with us — loving her children even in disagreement. After speaking in generalities, I finally began to tell her about a specific situation I was facing. Mother agreed that I was in a difficult position. Daddy did not say a word, but because of his failing hearing, I assumed he either couldn't follow the conversation or wasn't interested in what we were saying.

Afterward, I walked with Daddy from the kitchen toward the long, brick hallway leading to his room. I could see light streaming in through the hallway's glass wall. My father was moving slowly, leaning on his walker, and as we got to the threshold of the brick floor, he stopped, indicating he wanted to tell me something about the conversation I had just had with Mother. He paused and looked straight into my eyes. Then with a voice full of conviction, referring to the

child with whom I was struggling, he said: "They're trying to do the right thing. And you need to support them."

I did not know what to say. Here was my father once again challenging me to go higher in my love for others. I was awed by his consistency. In so many words, he was pushing me to extend the same grace to my child that he had extended to me in the kitchen those years ago when, devastated by my own mistakes, I had read him that letter to my husband. Could I now look at my child and say those same words: "We all live under grace and do the best we can"? Could I offer the same love my father offered me when, not agreeing with what I had done, he embraced me in the driveway and said, "Welcome home"?

Standing with Daddy now, I was struck by my own failure to see what he saw — that my child was trying to do the right thing. I had always thought I had a handle on grace. I have made many mistakes in my life. I have fallen down. I have sinned. I have needed an overwhelming amount of grace, and that grace has been given to me when I did not deserve it, which, of course, is what makes it grace.

Because I have received grace myself, I thought I could extend grace easily to others — I assumed I would always be quick to say: *It's all right. God loves you. Go to him and ask for forgiveness. He will not abandon you.* But here I was at home with my parents, discussing a difficult situation, which, in fact, was an opportunity to offer grace to my own child, and I did not see it. It took my father, in his gentle way, speaking a simple truth there in the bright hallway, for me to understand what God wanted from me. God wanted grace. He wanted compassion. He wanted what he himself had given to me. And by holding up my father's perspective as a gauge — or, more than his perspective, the character of Christ formed in him — God graciously showed me what I lacked and gave me the opportunity to change.

Me with two of my grandchildren, Wyatt and Virginia Ruth

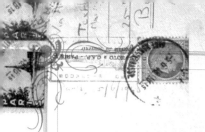

- CHAPTER FIVE -

# Loyalty

*Behold, how good and how pleasant it is*
*For brothers to dwell together in unity!*

PSALM 133:1 NASB

L ast Thursday when my wife, Ruth, told me over the phone, I was at the Mayo Clinic in Jacksonville, Florida, where I'd been for a number of weeks."

Daddy is speaking in a low, solemn tone. He has just stepped into the pulpit at First Baptist Church in Swannanoa, North Carolina, a small mountain town between Asheville and Montreat. A moment ago, Franklin introduced Daddy saying, briefly, "I was asked to introduce my father … and that's kind of … you know.… Daddy, you come."

Those seated, many of my father's closest friends, laughed as he rose and made his way to the pulpit where he now stands speaking. Though we are here to say good-bye to a man we loved, we have also come to celebrate — Uncle T. W. Wilson has gone home to be with the Lord.

The sanctuary is packed this afternoon. I am sitting in the second row; my siblings Anne and Franklin are seated in front of me. George Beverly Shea, "Uncle Bev," now in his nineties, is beside them; he will be getting up to sing soon. Next to him is Uncle Cliff Barrows, in his late seventies. Behind me are the families and friends of my father's team members, and many others who loved Uncle T.

Daddy continues with his talk, sharing about the phone call he got at Mayo's from Mother: "And she told me that T. W. had just gone to heaven. I was first in a state of shock. But then I began to rejoice. Because I found that he had beaten me to heaven." Now Daddy looks up with a boyish grin. Laughter rises. He goes on, keeping to his notes.

"And we'd often talked about that—who'd go next? Especially since his brother Grady had gone on to be with the Lord several years ago. We'd often talked about the future life and what it was going to be like when we got there. And we talked about the friends we'd be seeing up there and the wonderful fellowship we were going to have when we get there. And he beat me there so I'm looking for him to welcome me when I get there, which I don't think will be too long—by that I mean the next fifty years."

Now the crowded church bursts into laughter, which seems to fit a celebration for Uncle T, a man who, with his ski jump nose, was often said to resemble Bob Hope, and who had a great sense of humor himself. He was always ready with a joke or a funny story; at the same time, he was just as ready to share a spiritual insight or to pray with whomever he met. In his warmth, he drew a big circle of people, but he could be a formidable foe if one of his loved ones was attacked.

I watch Daddy's facial expressions as he talks — somber then light-hearted, always loving. He talks of Uncle T being a servant, an encourager, and an evangelist.

He talks of Uncle T's love of the Bible. Of his being a "man of prayer." Of how much he misses Uncle T.

I miss him too. I remember how affectionate he was with me — always telling me he was proud of me, and that he loved me, treating me like a daughter. Looking across the sanctuary now, I see his own daughter, Sally, one of my best friends growing up, sitting in a pew nearby, listening attentively. I remember the times in our girlhood spent together with our fathers — a drive up the California coast one summer; a winter weekend in Key Biscayne. Uncle T adored his children. He treated them like they were the greatest children that had ever been born. And he loved us — Daddy's children. He was totally devoted to my father, as was my father to him.

Daddy grew up with Grady and T. W. Wilson in Charlotte, North Carolina. Their families knew each other, but their personal friendship was cemented during the 1934 Mordecai Ham evangelistic meetings where Daddy, as a teenager, gave his life to Christ. The three young men ended up in a Bible study together, and shortly thereafter they all became traveling salesmen for the Fuller Brush Company. Daddy's succinct description of the teenage T. W. was "burly." Always a big man, Uncle T, even when young, could have passed for a bouncer, Daddy wrote.[1]

George Beverly Shea ("Uncle Bev"), Uncle Cliff, and "Uncle Tedd" Smith

It was Grady who first joined Daddy and Uncle Cliff in their evangelistic campaigns. He left a pastorate to become part of the team, coming on board full-time after the 1949 Greater Los Angeles meetings, which thrust my father's ministry into the national spotlight. Grady's title was associate evangelist, but he wore many hats — serving my father as a traveling companion, assistant, confidant, advisor, and BGEA board member. T. W. came to the team later, also giving up a pastorate and eventually his own evangelistic meetings to serve as an associate evangelist and a kind of chief-of-staff. Among other duties, he managed the Montreat office, traveled with Daddy, often oversaw security, and served on the BGEA board. T. W. was like a brother to my father. Both he and Grady, along with Cliff Barrows, George Beverly Shea, Tedd Smith, George Wilson, Esther LaDow, Charlie Riggs, Russ Busby, and Walter Smyth formed the core of Daddy's ministry team. Those still living and not retired continue on with Daddy in some capacity today.

Sitting in the pew at the church in Swannanoa, I look up at Daddy now — at his shock of white hair, his blue eyes — as he stands in the pulpit talking. Then I glance over at Uncle Bev and Uncle Cliff; they seem thoughtful, introspective. I think, here are these old warhorses gathering together to say good-bye to their friend. And look at them: Uncle Bev is still singing. Uncle Cliff is still leading others in song. Daddy is still preaching. Even when talking about Uncle T, he preaches gently. Here they are at their friend's funeral, honoring their own, and still doing what God has called them to do. As they pass on one by one — first Uncle Grady, then Uncle George Wilson, now Uncle T; Uncle Walter Smyth would go later — those who remain celebrate and anticipate the passing themselves.

"We'd often talked about the future life," Daddy had said of T. W. at the beginning of his eulogy. These men who have served God faithfully together in life now talk of being together forever. That is sweetness. That is loyalty. That is love.

DADDY, UNCLE T, UNCLE CLIFF, AND
"UNCLE GRADY" WILSON, 1987

## Old Warhorses

Four years after Uncle T's funeral, as I sat in the blazing sun at Flushing Meadows Corona Park in New York City for the last day of what was billed as my father's final crusade in America — it ended up being the final crusade of his career — I was struck by a similar impression. It was June 2005. The phrase that kept playing in my mind was the same that struck me at the church in Swannanoa: "old warhorses." Here they were again — Daddy, Uncle Bev, and Uncle Cliff — together again, this time for another kind of good-bye. A good-bye to the work of the ministry they had known from their youth.

At age ninety-six, Uncle Bev got up in the blistering afternoon heat and, leaning on one side of Daddy's pulpit, sang "How Great Thou Art" to a crowd of some ninety thousand people; while Uncle Cliff, standing on the opposite side of the pulpit, directed the enormous choir positioned behind the platform, bringing them in to join Uncle Bev for the hymn's chorus. Afterward, Daddy went forward, leaning on his walker — with Franklin standing by to get him situated in his pulpit — and he preached a message called "When Christ Comes Again." Here were the three men doing what they had done so often, now for the final time.

Before he began to preach, Daddy took a moment to acknowledge his two friends. First, he thanked some elected officials, the press, and those involved in organizing the crusade. Then he spoke of his beloved team members, and as he did, all I could think of was the lifetime of commitment these men had shown one another in service to God.

"But especially — especially," Daddy said with feeling, " — I want to thank my longtime friends and associates who have put up with me so many years — sixty years we've been together: Cliff Barrows and George Beverly Shea."

With the mention of the two men, the enormous audience in the park began to applaud. Seated on the platform next to each other, Uncle Cliff and Uncle Bev clasped hands for a moment as Daddy went on: "They are two of the greatest men of God I have ever known." Now the applause escalated, and my father encouraged it, adding, "That's right." The crowd stood to its feet, as Uncle Cliff and Uncle Bev remained seated, looking out over the vast audience, their faces soft with emotion.

In a moment, my father motioned to them, and they went to stand beside him. Daddy's microphone picked up the conversation. "It's been a privilege," said Uncle Bev, his eyes bright, as he reached over the pulpit ledge and shook Daddy's hand.

Uncle Cliff then grasped my father's right arm and said, smiling, "It really has, buddy."

Uncle Bev, Uncle Cliff, and Daddy in New York, 2005

## Team Loyalty

Though the media came out to the New York crusade largely to see my father — we were told that the press conference he gave the day before the meetings was one of the largest in the city's history — Daddy wasn't going to take the limelight for himself. The limelight belonged to God. Beyond that my father has always talked of himself as part of a group of people committed body, mind, and soul to the work God gave them to do — the work of evangelism. My father was the leader, but the ministry has never been a one-man show; and Daddy doesn't like it to be cast that way.

Speaking of Uncle Cliff and Uncle Bev at the press conference, my father said, "I have some wonderful associates that come with me [to the meetings]." Then he added, "Or, I go with them." The way my father reversed his statement says it all. The ministry is not his ministry; it is a team effort. The team goes with him, he goes with the team — it is all the same. They go to their engagements together.

Not only has the ministry been a team effort, but what strikes me is that it has also been an effort made largely by the same team. Looking at a 1964 photograph of BGEA associate evangelists in *Just As I Am*, I can name only one man in the group who left the team and went on to do other things later in life. The others are either still part of the ministry, or they stayed on until they died.

For as long as I can remember, I've seen the loyalty of my father's team operate in the most intimate settings. The Christmas I was pregnant with my first child, for instance, I was not able to travel and missed out on celebrating the holidays with my family. Instead, my husband, Ted, and I spent Christmas in nearby Philadelphia with his parents, Fred and Millie Dienert, longtime associates and friends of my parents. I remember something "Uncle Fred"—as I always knew him—said to me in the course of conversation. Trying to comfort me over the missed trip to Montreat, he began talking about his love for my parents, emphasizing how much he loved Daddy. He looked me in the eye, and, as if it were the most natural thing in the world, he said, "I would give my life for your father."

Right then I knew Uncle Fred's remark was more than a statement designed to comfort me—it was the truth. Uncle Fred loved my father. And Daddy loved and depended on him. Even today my father often talks about Fred Dienert, who passed away in 1993. Now and then when I am at home, Daddy will look at me wistfully and say, "I miss Fred."

## LEADING WITH LOYALTY

As long as he has been in ministry, something about my father has engendered the fierce loyalty of others. Perhaps it is partly Daddy's graciousness and acceptance of people. He is not judgmental, as he has demonstrated in my own life at critical times. Coming to my father, you do not feel like you're approaching a judge, but a friend and ally. President George W. Bush expressed this same impression, writing in his autobiography, "Billy Graham didn't make you feel guilty; he made you feel loved."[2]

Perhaps it is Daddy's passionate love for Christ that prompts people to commit their lives to working alongside him. Or the broad vision he serves in taking the gospel to the world. Or his unyielding devotion to the work. Perhaps it is his integrity, or his humility. All of these qualities make Daddy a leader worth following. But my father also demonstrates unwavering loyalty to those who walk with him; and I think as much as anything, it is his love for and commitment to those who serve him that makes him an effective leader.

Daddy's relationship with longtime BGEA associate evangelist John Wesley White poignantly illustrates my father's commitment to his colleagues. A Canadian with a tremendous intellect, John has a depth of knowledge of the Scriptures I have rarely seen. Over the course of his career as an evangelist, he held numerous crusades of his own in Canada and the United States; he also served my father in the areas of research and writing.

Beyond large-scale ministry, John took a special interest in our family. He was the first person to invite my brother Franklin to preach, and he went on to encourage and mentor Franklin in ministry. After my second marriage fell apart, John asked me to come to one of his meetings in Ontario and share my testimony. I felt unworthy, inadequate, and ill-qualified to be giving my testimony after the way I had messed up my life; but John must have seen something in me, because he didn't shy away from my brokenness — he encouraged me while I was in it.

In these and many other ways, John served my father faithfully from the 1960s. Then in 1996, in his sixties, he suffered a massive stroke that at first left him barely able to speak. As he gained a measure of recovery, he began writing (and still writes) encouraging letters to Daddy and other friends and colleagues — called "The White Papers," the letters contain biblical teaching and insights on world events. Eventually, John was able to travel again, and my father started sending him and his wife, Kathleen, to BGEA crusades so they could continue to be part of the ministry. Whatever his limitations, John was still a valuable team member, and my father stood by him. He didn't pass over John because of a physical setback. Quite the opposite, Daddy still counted on John — on his insights, support, and prayers. And he loves John. He remains faithful to his friend, returning loyalty to one who has demonstrated a lifetime of loyalty to him.

## DIVIDED LOYALTY

I have always known my father as someone who keeps lifelong friends. He doesn't drop people. Despite his scheduling restrictions, I have watched him work hard over the years to maintain his relationships. He uses the means available, as he did with us when we were growing up, sending letters and gifts, calling, and visiting when possible. Even now, as limited as he is, he still travels to Charlotte to spend time with his sisters and cousins and their families. He has every excuse not to go, but he makes the trip — because he is a man who loves deeply.

Considering my father's heart for others, I see more clearly just how large a sacrifice he made to follow God's call in ministry. For a man who loves as my father does, to be away from those he loved must have been intensely painful, even as he has said. At times he must have felt robbed of family experiences, excluded from intimacy, and lonely. From this perspective, deciding to do his best with the work and trust God — as he constantly advised me to do — must have been a matter of emotional survival. And I can imagine that leaving us in God's hands while wanting to take care of us himself probably left my father constantly divided. On the one hand was his loyalty to the call of God; on the other, his loyalty to family and loved ones. I'm sure the number of times he had to choose between family and ministry is too high to count.

My grandparents, L. Nelson and Virginia Bell

My daughter, Noelle, and me, 1974

One dramatic illustration of the struggle my father faced stands out in memory. The circumstance was the death of my grandmother, Virginia Bell, in November 1974.

I was twenty-three with an eleven-month-old child when we lost *Lao Niang*, as we called her, using our own version of the Chinese for grandmother. *Lao Niang* was Mother's mother; as I've shared, she and my grandfather, Nelson Bell — whom we called *Lao E* — spent nearly twenty-five years as medical missionaries in China. During World War II, they were forced to leave the country, and they ended up settling in Montreat, where Mother and Daddy also settled as a young married couple. If my father was going to travel, Mother said, then she wanted to be near her parents. Until their deaths, *Lao E* and *Lao Niang* lived at the bottom of our mountain.

We lost my grandfather first, in 1973, and Mother suffered greatly. We all did, being so close to him. But losing *Lao Niang* the following autumn was, for me, a trauma. Just the month before — in October — when visiting my sister Gigi and her family in Milwaukee, Mother had suffered a terrifying fall that left her critically injured. Ever unpredictable, she had taken it upon herself to have some fun with her grandchildren, running a line between two trees and attaching a pipe so the kids could grab hold of the pipe and slide down. Wanting to give the slide a test run, Mother climbed a tree to get to the top of the line, took hold of the pipe, and promptly fell fifteen feet when the line broke. She shattered her heel, compressed her spine, broke a rib, and blacked out, falling into a coma for a week.

It was while she was recovering at Gigi's that Mother learned *Lao Niang* had suffered a stroke. Mother was still physically fragile. Nevertheless, on crutches and struggling with memory loss, she flew home to Montreat to be with her mother. I met her there, and we had *Lao Niang* moved from the hospital in Asheville to her own house, where she continued to fail. Not long afterward, on November 8, she passed away. We expected it but were still hit hard. Daddy was in Norfolk, Virginia, at the time, holding a crusade.

At first, my father was not going to come home for *Lao Niang's* funeral. The timing was bad — he was wrapping up the ten-day crusade in Virginia's Tidewater area — and as I understood, people were pressuring Daddy that the work of the Lord would be hindered if he left Norfolk. Daddy, I am certain, was torn over the decision, but he made the choice he thought best — to stay in Norfolk — and we resigned ourselves to it.

Our family pastor, Calvin Thielman, who lived in Montreat, on the other hand, was not settled with my father's decision. Intimately acquainted with our circumstances, he stepped in and called Daddy.

I do not know what was said, but my father changed his mind and made plans to come home.

Daddy stayed with us in Montreat for my grandmother's funeral, and his presence brought some relief. Still, I knew he was planning to leave before the burial, and this did not seem right to me. In Mother's biography, *A Time for Remembering*, author Patricia Daniels Cornwell describes Mother at the funeral as "dizzy, swinging perilously down the aisle on crutches."[3] Later we learned she had no memory of the service. I needed my father to stay with us. I needed his help and comfort. I needed him to be at home with Mother. I had stood vigil with Mother beside *Lao Niang*'s bed, and there, for the first time ever, I had seen my mother cry. Watching her grieve, especially in her debilitated physical condition, greatly disturbed me. I felt inadequate to comfort her. How could my father leave us at a time like this?

As he was packing up to go, I went back to Daddy's bedroom. I knew he was leaving. I knew there was nothing I could do. But I wanted to speak up. For the first time — and the only time that I can remember — I asked him why. "Why can't you stay with us?" I asked through my tears. "How can you leave?"

Daddy was somewhat abrupt. He put his arms around me, but he spoke firmly. "You'll understand one day," he said. And that was the end of the conversation. He was going. He needed to get ready. The matter was settled. I needed to trust him, and I tried. But my heart was not pacified.

From where I sit now, I must admit I still do not understand how my father could have left us in those circumstances. We had lost our grandmother. Our mother was on crutches and had been in a coma. We were all grieving. And Daddy went back to the crusade. It was a hard time. At least for me.

And yet I realize how difficult that decision must have been for Daddy. It could not have been easy leaving his family in that condition. And to have me come to him weeping, asking him to stay, must have been very painful. Here he was forced to choose between family and ministry at a critical time for both. He had made such choices on countless occasions. Perhaps over the years the choice had become easier. Maybe not. I don't know. But this time his family's need was so pronounced, he had to have suffered. And on the other side people were telling him the work of God would be set back if he left the crusade — what a horrible burden! I'm sure my father tried to balance his loyalty both to the ministry and to us as best he could. I don't know how he felt. But it must have been tough for him.

On a much smaller scale, I feel the same kind of pull in my own life at times: I have ministry demanding my attention, and I have grown children with young families who need me. This last summer we all spent time together at the beach. I chose to use my mornings for ministry work and give the afternoons to my children. One of the children expressed frustration over the arrangement — she said she felt shortchanged. I was frustrated too. I couldn't give a hundred percent to either my family or the ministry. My loyalty was divided.

WITH MY FAMILY, SUMMER 2005

I try my best to balance everything, but ministry does tend to demand more time and energy. Unfortunately, family often seems to offer the least resistance — which means I must be extra vigilant in guarding those relationships, even in small ways. For example, I send postcards to my nine-year-old grandson, Wyatt, from the different cities I visit to let him know I'm thinking of him and to give him a little history or geography lesson. Recently, from Atlanta, Georgia, I sent him a postcard of Martin Luther King Jr., explaining that Dr. King was a friend of "Daddy Bill's" (as the grandchildren and great-grandchildren call my father) and a man who changed the course of history.

I suppose I'm putting into practice some of the habits my father developed as he navigated the family-ministry divide — reaching out to loved ones through letters, notes, and phone calls. Still, thinking about Daddy from my current perspective, it is sometimes difficult to believe he survived the heartbreak of the divide, especially during his family's early years when his children were young and his marriage new. The older I get the more impressed I am with my father's perseverance, and the more saddened by the weight he had to bear.

## Handling Betrayal

Even as my father has experienced lasting, mutual loyalty in ministry, like most leaders — perhaps every leader — he has also known betrayal. What stands out is the way he has handled it. Daddy does not answer his critics. He takes the high road. His caution to me about criticizing others — his grace-filled approach to people generally — also applies to those who have wronged him. If someone hurts him, Daddy gives that person the benefit of the doubt. He doesn't even allow his own family to pass judgment.

I remember a particular conversation that took place at my grandparents' house in Montreat when I was a child. As I recall, my father, grandparents, and I had gathered in the pine-paneled living room, overlooking the front lawn and a side yard where *Lao Niang* often hosted little tea parties for my sister Anne and me. I could see the front lawn reflected in the mirror over the fireplace. The mantel clock chimed, and the adults talked among themselves, as I sat on the floor searching for pieces of a game we had been playing.

My grandfather sat in his rocking chair; Daddy was in the corner chair. They were discussing difficulties my father had experienced in a relationship with a friend with whom he had worked closely. It seemed to me this friend had been publicly critical of Daddy, and that my father was asking my grandfather for advice on how to handle the

situation. Their voices showed concern. I don't recall the specifics. It may have been they were talking about Charles Templeton, once a fellow Youth for Christ (YFC) evangelist who worked with my father; or perhaps they were speaking of someone else. In the case of Chuck Templeton, Daddy has written in his memoir about what happened.

After Chuck Templeton and my father toured Great Britain and Europe on a 1946 YFC preaching campaign, Chuck left the church he was pastoring and enrolled at Princeton Theological Seminary. There he found himself struggling with spiritual questions, particularly concerning the authority of the Bible; and he and my father discussed these issues in depth.

My father, who was reading a range of theologians at the time, found himself similarly confused, likewise wrestling with questions about the Scriptures' authority. "My respect and affection for Chuck were so great," Daddy wrote, "that whatever troubled him troubled me also."[4]

This struggle over the Scriptures — whether they were divinely inspired and could be taken and trusted as the Word of God — plagued my father for some time. By now he was serving as president of Northwestern Schools, which was a liberal arts college, Bible school, and seminary. He was also an evangelist on the cusp of the 1949 Los Angeles meetings, which would launch his ministry into another dimension. And here he was facing questions that rocked the very foundation of what he believed he was called to do. He had hit a low point, a critical valley of decision.

Just before the Los Angeles Campaign was set to begin in September 1949, my father attended a conference at Forest Home, a retreat center near the city. Chuck Templeton attended too, and they continued their conversations about theological issues.

"Billy," Chuck said to my father, "you're fifty years out of date. People no longer accept the Bible as being inspired the way you do. Your faith is too simple." Later, a friend of Daddy's overheard Chuck say, "Poor Billy, I feel sorry for him. He and I are taking two different roads."[5]

These remarks wounded my father — cut him to the quick, as he put it. Chuck was a friend and one he esteemed. And yet, as hurt as Daddy was, it was the deeper struggle within his own heart over the Scriptures that occupied him. One night at the retreat, burdened with his lack of clarity, my father went out for a walk. "Could I trust the Bible?" he wondered. "With the Los Angeles Campaign galloping toward me, I had to have an answer. If I *could not* trust the Bible, I could not go on."[6]

Out in the woods, my father stopped, got down on his knees,

and opened up his Bible, placing it on a tree stump. There he made a decision that sealed his life's course. He prayed, telling God that even though he didn't understand the Bible's "seeming contradictions," even though he still had questions, he was going to believe it by faith as the Word of God. "I am going to allow faith to go beyond my intellectual questions and doubts," he told God, "and I will believe this to be Your inspired Word."[7]

When he got up, Daddy felt the peace of God, and he knew that something had been settled — a spiritual battle "fought and won."[8]

Weeks later Los Angeles happened — two months of evangelistic meetings that changed my father and his ministry forever. Daddy called the retreat before the campaign "[o]ne of God's hidden stratagems to prepare me for Los Angeles."[9]

But even though the hurtful words of someone my father considered a friend spurred Daddy on to accept the Scriptures by faith as true and inspired, pain over the betrayal was real, and the two men eventually parted ways. Perhaps some of the circumstances surrounding this relationship were the subject of the adults' discussion that afternoon, years later, as I sat on the floor in my grandparents' living room. Perhaps the adults were referring to someone else. Either way, the response my father gave was characteristic.

Self-absorbed and not really understanding all that was being said, I grasped only that someone had hurt Daddy. This disturbed me; I didn't want anyone to think negatively of my father. Then one of the adults spoke up in defense of Daddy — probably my grandmother, who could be feisty — and I was glad.

But my father answered gently, speaking more to himself than to anyone else. "We shouldn't criticize," he said, looking down. "We don't know this person's heart or motives. We will let God handle it."

## LETTING GOD HANDLE IT

I have heard my father speak words like these time and again, and his actions follow suit: he lets God handle the opposition that comes against him; he doesn't try to take matters into his own hands. Though I'm sure it causes him pain and frustration, he maintains an attitude of grace — even protectiveness — toward his critics and enemies. When wounded, he refuses to harm the reputation of the one who inflicted the wound; he demonstrates a form of loyalty — and love, choosing to follow what Jesus commanded when he said, "love your enemies, bless those who curse you, do good to those who hate you, and pray for those who spitefully use you and persecute you" (Matthew 5:44 NKJV).

In fact, when Chuck Templeton was dying, my father went to visit him and prayed with him. Daddy had kept limited contact with his old friend over the years. Even though Chuck had criticized my father's work, Daddy still cared deeply for him. He loved Chuck and chose to see beyond the conflict. He could have easily written Chuck off and forgotten him, but he did not. He demonstrated love to one who hurt him, loving in spite of the betrayal.

Considering the whole of my father's character, his response to criticism and disloyalty is consistent with his response to people in most situations. I think back to the way he treated the strangers who approached him in public when I was a girl — never saying no, never turning people away, even when they interrupted our family meals. As much as his willingness to accommodate others might have frustrated me, as much as I felt cheated of precious family time, my father's generosity characterizes his responses to people in a wide range of scenarios, including betrayal.

Some of Daddy's reluctance to engage opponents could be due to a dislike of confrontation — I know this is true of me. I would much rather let things go than step up and confront someone. And yet there have been times in life when I've wanted to stand up to critics, fight back, and justify myself — or my family. In one of my Bibles from the 1970s, I marked some verses in Psalm 35 as a prayer for my father when I thought others were out to damage his reputation: "Contend, O LORD, with those who contend with me; Fight

against those who fight against me" (Psalm 35:1 NASB). My loyalty was with my folks, but I was trying to put into practice what I had seen my father model in the face of disloyalty. I was praying, turning my concerns over to God, and "letting God handle it."

Leaving fears, situations, and hurts with God can be a battle. Even as I prayed those verses from Psalm 35, I was struggling against anxiety over what might happen to my parents. I prayed through the worry until I felt peaceful. But sometimes peace doesn't come. I can pray and find myself still worried, still anxious. And in those instances, I have to make a decision to trust God in spite of my fears. Ultimately, this is what the battle turns on — trust. Do we trust God? Do we trust him to take care of us? Do we trust him to "handle it"?

So much that I've learned from my father seems to circle back around to these questions. Trusting God, depending on him, having faith in his goodness and love — this really is my father's legacy to me. Everything comes down to honest faith. As a young man kneeling in the woods one night with his Bible laid out on a tree stump; as a middle-aged man faced with his family's bereavement during an evangelistic campaign; as an elderly man speaking about heaven at the funeral of his beloved friend: whatever the challenge, faith has been the answer for my father. A legacy of faith is what he leaves me.

# Authenticity

*I have fought the good fight,*
*I have finished the course, I have kept the faith.*

2 TIMOTHY 4:7 NASB

On May 14, 2004, I was sitting in my living room with my sister Gigi and our childhood friend, Jane Frist — they had stopped to visit me in Virginia — when we got a phone call from Montreat. It was a friend of Jane's, calling to say she had heard an ambulance racing up the mountain toward my parents' house.

Immediately, we called the Montreat BGEA office. The folks there said that as far as they knew, my parents were fine. Soon afterward, though, we got the news. It came from Daddy's executive assistant, David Bruce; he was calling all of the children. Daddy had fallen, he said, and broken his pelvis.

We were dismayed. Daddy was just getting over a partial hip replacement after a fall earlier in the year. He had worked so hard to recover from that surgery, and now this — a major setback. Apparently, thinking he was stronger than he was, he had gotten up on his own, without the help of his nurse, and had fallen again.

Gigi, Jane, and I set out for home the following morning, and I went straight to Mission Hospitals in Asheville where my father was staying. When I got to his room, he was in some discomfort. He didn't look bad — his face was animated. In my journal I actually wrote, "Daddy looked great." But the fracture was serious, and a decision about what medical course to take had not yet been made. We were all anxious to hear what the doctor would advise.

I pulled up a chair next to my father's bed, and he began to talk about the future. Even in pain and uncertainty, he was thinking of his work. He was scheduled to preach at meetings in Kansas City the following month; and after that, at another crusade in Los Angeles; and later at yet another in New York. He wondered whether he would recover in time to make it to his engagements — or recover at all.

"Daddy," I said, reaching for his hand, "I'm so sorry you have to go through this." I hated to see him suffer and was concerned about the long recovery ahead.

But then, looking into his blue eyes, I was struck by something else: how peaceful he seemed, not at all anxious. I knew he was thinking about Kansas City and the other ministry dates. And yet his answer was not one of frustration or impatience, but of tranquility, a calm resignation.

"Well," he said, "I'm in the Lord's hands. If this is the way I am to end my career, then so be it."

I sat there and smiled, nodding my head in agreement. What he said — and the way he said it — impressed me. Others in his predicament might have asked, "Why me? I've just recovered from a broken hip. I've got this work to do. I don't have time for this." I probably would've been thinking that way. And maybe those thoughts did flash across Daddy's mind at some point. All I know is that by the time I got to him, in spite of his own hopes and desires, he was content, and totally accepting of whatever God had for him.

"I'm in God's hands," he had said.

*I'm in God's hands.* There was that trust again. Daddy's dependence on the Lord — his faith. My father loved and trusted the Lord so much that he knew God had a purpose for him even in this setback. Whatever God wanted really was fine with him.

Watching Daddy, looking into his eyes as he lay there, I realized anew just how authentic his faith was — it was the real thing; not something that only showed up when he was preaching to vast crowds. For even in his most private, painful moments — in this case, a limiting moment in old age — my father placed himself in God's hands. He didn't want to be there in the hospital; he wanted to be able to preach in Kansas City. But I didn't detect any resentment, any frustration. It was just, "If this is the way God wants me to end, then this is fine."

## JUST HIMSELF

Looking back, I don't remember ever sensing that my father was trying to maintain two images — public and private. With my father, what you see is what you get. Whatever the setting, he is just himself. And that is authenticity. Daddy has never been a fake. He is honest about his frailties — though, as I've shared, honest without being overly reflective. He is aware of his weaknesses. He will enumerate them. And then he moves on to the next thing: the work God has given him — evangelism.

Over his lifetime my father has remained remarkably consistent in his focus on evangelism, consistent in his mission — another mark of the authentic life. You pick up his preoccupation in his conversation; he always pulls talk around to God. If he makes an appearance on a talk show, regardless of the questions, he finds a way to turn conversation back to the gospel. If he is at home talking to local folk, he circles talk around to the gospel. Daddy doesn't waver. He can talk about faith to a president. He can talk about it to an alcoholic on the street. He focuses on God, and personal faith in Christ, whenever and wherever he can.

Now, when he is in the hospital, Daddy shares the gospel with everyone from the nurses and doctors to the maintenance staff. He is not giving a performance. He doesn't do it because sharing the gospel is expected of Billy Graham. He reaches out of himself to meet spiritual needs because that is who my father is. In the past, when Mother was the one in the hospital, and Daddy the one visiting, he would tend to get sidetracked praying with other patients, still facing the dilemma of divided loyalty. He would have been there after all to see Mother! But even this struggle is part of my father's consistency.

In the days after he broke his pelvis, I visited Daddy as often I could before having to return to Virginia. Knowing my father's reading interests, I went to the bookstore and picked up a biography of the president, thinking it might be a good distraction. Earlier in the year, after his previous fall and the partial hip replacement, Daddy spent much of his recovery time reading through a new translation of the Bible — the one in which he made no notes.

Daddy was appreciative of the book. "He is so tender," I wrote in my journal, "and a gentleman to the end — always courteous." In the same visit, he went on to discuss some of the details of his health with me, and, true to form, he apologized if he had embarrassed me. "He didn't [embarrass me]," I wrote, "but it made me aware of how frail and vulnerable he is.... It is so hard to see both of them [Mother and Daddy] so dependent."

And yet, even in his frailty my father was still wholly himself.

Still forward-looking, still hopeful, still passionate about his work should God allow him to continue to do it. There in that hospital bed my father could have made the decision to end his ministry career, and no one would have blamed him. But he was still the man he had been all of his life. The drive to keep going, the desire not to be waylaid, his heart for evangelism, his burden for the work — these were all operating in him even then, at his weakest. He was content to accept whatever the future held, but he was looking ahead to Kansas City and Los Angeles even so. He was praying for the people of those cities. And beyond those cities, he was looking toward New York.

## More Time

A few days after I arrived in Asheville to see my father, the doctor met with Mother and Daddy — and some of my siblings and me — and he laid out Daddy's options.

Mother was quiet during the discussion. My father wondered aloud if maybe God was closing the door on crusades for that year, or maybe forever. As currently scheduled, Kansas City was out for Daddy, a reality to which he quickly adjusted. Medical options were weighed, and the procedure eventually chosen involved placing pins in my father's pelvis to hold it together — a less-invasive option. The recovery would be long, but the general sentiment was that Daddy was in good condition and could recover. Mother talked of the quality of care my father could receive at home after his procedure. Watching her, I thought she might be concerned, even afraid, that Daddy wouldn't make it home at all. He was eighty-five, and we had just learned of a man my father's age who died of pneumonia in the hospital after breaking his pelvis.

But my father did make it home, and, staying disciplined in his physical therapy, he slowly recovered. God had given him more time. And more strength. My father preached in both Kansas City and Los Angeles — the crusade schedule was adjusted to accommodate him — and after those events, he began to get ready for the meetings in New York, pushed back by several months to late June 2005. It was decided that New York City would probably be Daddy's last crusade in the United States, perhaps his final crusade, though no one had made that decision. Either way, New York was billed and organized to be a grand finale in a decades-long ministry that had impacted generations around the world. To end in New York would be, in a sense, to have come full circle. As scheduled, the event would fall during the forty-eighth anniversary of my father's historic, months-long 1957 crusade in that city. And it was with this end in sight that Daddy, in between periods of rest, began his preparations.

UNCLE BEV AND DADDY, 2005 NEW YORK CRUSADE

## Authenticity in New York

If I have seen my father's authenticity shine anywhere, I saw it at the 2005 meetings in New York. The crusade marked the six-decade-plus span of his career — one he began in the thirties, preaching as a college student in Florida, before graduating eventually from Wheaton College; pastoring a church in the Chicago area; preaching in the United States and Europe with Youth for Christ; serving as president of Northwestern Schools; and launching his own citywide campaigns with meetings in Grand Rapids, Michigan, and his hometown of Charlotte in 1947.

Very few people on the international scene have been committed to one mission for sixty years. When you operate in your calling or role for that long, your authenticity, or lack thereof, is going to show. And at the 2005 crusade in New York, a bookend on my father's lifelong career as an evangelist, he showed himself to be true. The qualities I have respected in him all of my life were visible: his love for the world, his father's heart, his humility, grace, and loyalty. In New York, Daddy gave the ministry everything he had. He was full of life and fully himself.

For me, the crusade in New York started out with a slight mishap — but one that ended happily by the time the first evening service was over. Late in the afternoon that first day I

FLUSHING MEADOWS CORONA PARK, 2005 NEW YORK CRUSADE

connected with some friends, BGEA board members, and other family members and boarded a bus to Flushing Meadows Corona Park in Queens for the event. We left the hotel in Manhattan in plenty of time to get there — a cushion of hours. This was fortunate because somehow the bus got lost! Three hours later we were pulling into the parking area just as the service was about to begin. Leaving our anxious driver, we all raced backstage to meet Daddy so he could be photographed with a group of his grandchildren and great-grandchildren. Later we learned that our bus driver had gone forward in the service to receive Christ, a very joyful ending to that first night.

The atmosphere around my father backstage in New York was different than I had observed it at past meetings — the last crusade I had attended was in Charlotte nearly a decade earlier. Since New York was to be Daddy's grand finale, there was something of a "groupie" feel to things. Normally he had a room — in this case a tent — where he could receive guests before his meetings; but at Corona Park my father's time seemed less controlled, unlike in the days when Uncle T held the reins. Here people were milling around watching Daddy. Interviewers came and went. Of course, this event was historic, so the awe and celebration made sense — it was good to see so many family members and old friends.

But I also believed the meetings required a sense of reverence. And because I grew up with the message, "Do not interrupt or distract your father from his work," I thought I needed to operate with that mindset here. I caught Daddy's eye from afar, and he smiled a greeting, so he knew I was there — and that was important to me. But I didn't go over to hug or be near him, and I must admit I regret my reserve now. I wish I had been more forward, freer in approaching Daddy, and in bringing friends to meet him. I wanted to honor his needs and those of the ministry, but looking back on it, I think I'm a little jealous of those who were less restrained.

Sitting near the platform that evening with family and friends, I watched the program unfold as day turned to dusk. Cliff Barrows, eighty-two, took the mike, an enthusiastic master of ceremonies, as congenial and loving and as big a presence as ever. He led the congregation, and the massive choir seated behind the platform, in "All Hail the Power of Jesus' Name" — "one of Mr. Graham's favorite hymns," he announced. Then he introduced a couple of contemporary musical groups, interspersed with prayer, the offering, and a personal testimony; and led "Amazing Grace." As the crowd and choir sang, some men helped my father, leaning on his walker, out to the stage. By the end of the hymn, Daddy was getting seated on the platform, just to the side of his pulpit — a wooden podium that accommodates him sitting or standing.

Now it was time for Bev Shea to sing. But before introducing him, Uncle Cliff extended a special greeting to my mother back at home. The meetings were being broadcast on Christian radio stations across the country, he explained. "And down in Black Mountain, North Carolina, Mrs. Billy Graham is there listening and sharing in the service. Let's give her a great big welcome by radio, shall we? We're so happy, Ruth, that you're there. We're praying for you …"

I thought of Mother and the times she had traveled to be with Daddy. So often when we were young she had chosen to stay home with us rather than go; and now, when she was free from such responsibilities, she was physically limited, too frail to attend. It made me sad, but I was delighted technology made it possible for her to "be there" in New York. I knew she had been praying, keenly interested in all that was happening on the ground.

After greeting Mother, Uncle Cliff announced it was time to welcome "America's beloved singer of sacred song," and George Beverly Shea made his way over to the side of Daddy's empty pulpit, supporting himself by resting his hand on the edge. He began

DADDY PREACHING, NEW YORK, 2005

by encouraging the audience with a spoken introductory lyric: "We can only see a little of the ocean as we stand on the rocky shore; but out there beyond the horizon, there's more, there's more." Then, in his rich, round voice, he led into a hymn, "The Love of God."

Noticing Daddy on the big screen during the hymn, I thought he looked wistful, melancholy maybe. Or perhaps he was simply focusing on what he had to do, feeling the weight of his mission. I remembered what he had written in his memoir about evangelistic preaching taking so much out of him: "I am constantly driving for commitment," he wrote. And: "[S]peaking of matters with eternal consequences is a great responsibility." And: "Preaching also involves us in a spiritual battle with the forces of evil."[1] Watching my father from my seat, I began to pray. I prayed that his strength would hold — that his body and his voice would hold out under the weight.

## Authentic Humility

As Uncle Bev finished, Daddy got up with his walker, and with Franklin's help, made his way to his pulpit. The crowd, on its feet, began cheering and applauding wildly. My father situated himself, standing inside the pulpit with his hands on the wooden sides, smiling a little sheepishly. Then he said in a low, sweet tone, "Thank you," and began.

There was my father: dark suit; white mane of hair; clear eyes; a tall, imposing frame, even in old age. He greeted the crowd and talked of his love for New York, thanking the people who had come. Then he shared a story I had heard many times, telling the crowd that he felt a little bit like he did years ago in Philadelphia, when a man boarded his elevator and said, "I hear Billy Graham is on here."

"Yes," my father's companion is said to have replied, pointing at Daddy, "there he is." To which the man, getting on board, said, "My, what an anticlimax!"

Gazing out across Corona Park with an earnest, apologetic expression, my father said, "And after all this music and all that you've read and heard, I'm sure that I'm an anticlimax."

Immediately, a sustained "No!" rose up from the audience. "Nooo!"

But knowing Daddy, he wasn't sharing the story about the man on the elevator in search of affirmation for himself — using that illustration was a genuine expression of his humility. He wanted people to focus not on him, but on God. As he went on to say later, at the end of the service after many came forward to give their hearts to Christ, "You've come tonight not to Billy Graham … not to Cliff Barrows or anybody like that. You've come to Jesus. And Jesus loves you; he forgives you. You've come to the cross."

What my father said to the crowd that night through the elevator story he has also expressed in various ways at home. Often I have heard my father, prompted by a question or conversation, share his doubt that he holds much influence in today's world. He seems to feel he has passed off the scene, though my experience bears out a vastly different reality. As I travel the country for my own ministry, people constantly approach me and tell me how much they love Daddy, commonly naming the date and city of the crusade where they gave their lives to Christ.

Regardless, my father does not make remarks about passing off the scene due to any apparent sense of insecurity, or need for recognition. When my father talks like this, he is matter-of-fact in his tone, unconcerned — and he is not saying anything new. These are the sorts of authentic expressions I have heard all my life. Consistently Daddy has spoken as a man who does not see

himself as entitled, or as anything special; but only as the common, North Carolina farmer's kid whom God simply chose. And that is how he came to the people in New York.

2005 NEW YORK PRESS CONFERENCE, ROCKEFELLER CENTER

The response of the crowd to Daddy's "anticlimax" story was a reflection of the greater response to my father's presence in New York and to the work of the ministry there. As Daddy said when he got up to preach the last service of the crusade on Sunday afternoon, he believed media coverage of the event represented the most extensive reporting on evangelism in New York that he had ever seen.

I was standing on the periphery of the room the day my father held his press conference in Rockefeller Center. Crammed in with hundreds of journalists, I was amazed at the respect they afforded my father. Reporters were so deferential as they asked questions, and people genuinely seemed honored to be in the room with him.

Daddy sat at a low table in front of a microphone and bantered with the press as he faced the wall of cameras and flash bulbs. Talking about the movement of world history, the premise for one of his messages, he said, "I'm glad that at the end of it all the Bible says that Jesus is coming back to this earth, and someday he is going to reign, and there'll be no tears, no suffering, no death ... a wonderful future; and I hope I'll meet all of you there, and bring your camera, because I may have one too!"

Laughter broke out as Daddy said this, and he seemed relaxed.

But he told me later he was nervous, feeling the weight of responsibility for the influence he carried speaking before the press. He didn't want to misstate anything about the Lord, or bring shame to God, which is always his burden when he gets up to preach. I thought back to what he told me in Montreat about preparing for ministry. He said he prays asking the Holy Spirit to help him, and sometimes "Lord, help!" is all he can say. When a reporter at the press conference asked him to share his favorite prayer, he answered the same way: "There's hardly a moment goes by that I don't pray, and I say, 'Lord, help me!' That's my favorite prayer."

More laughter rose with this answer, and that was remarkable to me. Everyone in the room, whatever their faith, seemed able to identify with that simple prayer. Because what my father was saying was not religious — it was real. We need help. We need God's help. Our cry for help may be the most basic expression of who we really are — *helpless* without the Lord, totally dependent on him. Whether we know it or not, we need God. And my father's understanding of this truth — the way he has lived it out — is worth more to me perhaps than all the messages he has preached. His *life* of faith in God — out of sheer desperation and need *leaning* on God, depending on God's help — is the greater message. It is the legacy of faith he leaves me.

## GOD'S LOVE

Watching Daddy preach in New York that June weekend in 2005, I had the overwhelming sense that I was looking at a battle-worn veteran — scarred, weathered, but undaunted. And, really, nothing about his message had changed; *fundamentally* nothing had changed. He still believed in the Word of God and the centrality of the cross of Christ. He was still preaching on the love of God, repentance for sin, forgiveness through the blood of Jesus, and the necessity of a personal relationship with God.

"The message that I preach here … hasn't changed," Daddy told the packed room of reporters at the press conference that Thursday afternoon. "Circumstances have changed. Problems have changed, but deep inside man has not changed, and the gospel hasn't changed."

If anything had changed about my father's preaching in New York, it might have been the delivery — it has become softer, gentler in his later years — and his emphasis seems to be ever more centered on the love of God. At the press conference he said he was going to refuse to answer questions he might have answered twenty years ago and simply focus on the gospel. "[A]t my age, … I have one message," he said.

When Larry King on his prime-time program asked Daddy

what he thought about Christian preachers making statements about non-Christians being condemned to "live in hell," Daddy went straight back to his message: "My calling is to preach the love of God and the forgiveness of God and the fact that he does forgive us. That's what the cross is all about, what the resurrection is all about, that's the gospel."

Daddy's own love, his graciousness, his welcome to people of all stripes, his open arms — I saw these qualities in full force in New York. He often talked of the mixture of ethnicities, nationalities, races, and faiths represented in the neighborhoods around Corona Park. When Larry King asked him how he felt about people of different faiths, Daddy said, "I love them all, and welcome them all, and love to be with them, and friends with all of them."

I think the consistency of my father's inclusive love over the years — even going back to his refusal to segregate his crusades in the South beginning in the 1950s — is something people have come to respect as authentic. I would argue that with age my father has become even more universal in his acceptance of others. He has come to a place where he transcends differences, boundaries, and divisions and just embraces people. As he told Larry King, he loves them all.

In a book released shortly after the crusade called *The Leadership Secrets of Billy Graham*, the last chapter, "Leading with Love," highlights an answer Daddy gave in a *20/20* interview. The interviewer asked him, "If you had a homosexual child, would you love him?" And Daddy's response, which moves me deeply, was immediate. "Why," he said, "I would love that one even more."[2]

## AUTHENTIC VALUES

My father has remained true in ministry to more than just the message — he and his team have implemented the *principles* of the message at an organizational level, giving the ministry a depth of authenticity that has caused the BGEA's efforts to flourish. Dr. A. R. Bernard, chairman of the 2005 Greater New York Crusade, spoke on the first evening, making reference to the core values that my father, Cliff Barrows, Bev Shea, and Grady Wilson established in 1948 during the ministry's infancy.

Sometimes called the "Modesto Manifesto," these core values grew out of what the men saw as the pitfalls of evangelism — financial corruption, sexual immorality, an anti-local-church attitude, and exaggerated accounts of success. The values the group came up with in response were integrity, accountability, purity of lifestyle, and humility. "They covenanted together," Dr. Bernard explained, "that these four core values would be the driving force behind their personal lives and the life of the Graham organization. They kept that covenant for more than fifty years."

He went on to say that the team's faithfulness in staying true to their values and message, coupled with the grace of God, is what has caused the ministry to last. I would agree. The work has been tested by time and shown to be authentic. And if there is any proof, it can be found in the response. People in Corona Park responded to the gospel, with so many making commitments to Christ, just as people have been making commitments since the ministry's first days. Of course, the response reflects the authenticity of the gospel message; but I also believe that to some extent, the response reflects the authenticity of the messenger and his team. If my father were some "Elmer Gantry," the bawdy caricature of an evangelist created by author Sinclair Lewis, then people would not have kept coming. But they have come — for sixty years.

The last meeting of the crusade took place on a blazing Sunday afternoon. The heat, the scorching sun, the humidity — these were tough to endure. There were no clouds, no shade to be found, no breeze. Just sun. But people came.

Partway through the program, my father and Uncle Bev came onto the platform while the choir sang "The Solid Rock." Daddy took his seat. There he was with his white hair, tanned face, black suit, and big black sunglasses — a striking figure.

Then Uncle Cliff introduced Uncle Bev and asked him to say a word of greeting. Uncle Bev noted that normally he never said a word of greeting before singing, but then he went ahead. "I was thirty-seven years old when I went with Mr. Graham," he said, "and now I'm ninety-six." The crowd applauded, presumably over the breadth of Uncle Bev's commitment and career. Then he added, nonchalantly, "And that means I'm almost through it," and launched right into the hymn he helped make famous, "How Great Thou Art," speaking the first two lines and finally opening up his deep bass voice with "I see the stars, I hear the rolling thunder ..."

As I looked on, taking it all in, my friend Sara Dormon, seated next to me, leaned over and asked, "How does this make you feel, knowing this is the last time this will happen?"

I had been moving so fast all weekend I hadn't paused to think about it. Here I was watching such a familiar event for the last time. This was the last time the three of them would work together like this: Uncle Cliff announcing and leading, Uncle Bev singing, and Daddy preaching. My father and the team had been invited to London, and they had not yet decided whether to accept the invitation, so when he got up to speak that day, Daddy left the possibility open for more. But I was thinking in terms of this being the last time for the team, so I tried to savor the moment. It made me a little weepy.

I also became aware of something my mother had said — her statement passed through my mind as I listened to Uncle Bev. She said, "Nothing of the work of God dies when a man of God dies." And the same is true, I believe, for a man who retires. God's work is going to go on. Though his servants come and go, the work of God lives.

Sitting there I comforted myself with that thought: God's work was going to continue. Not in the same venue, not in the same way, not in the same pattern. My father's was a unique ministry. What God would choose to do with it in the future I did not know; but my father, Uncle Cliff, and Uncle Bev probably would not be ministering together this way anymore. And that was sad.

Still, I had the sense too that it was time. Endings are part of life, aren't they? The flower blooms in spring, but death comes in the fall. It's all just part of life.

## PEACE WITH GOD

My father had a wonderful time in New York — he was energized and seemed to grow stronger each evening. Afterward, he went to Mayo's to recuperate and then headed home to Montreat. He and the organization made the decision not to accept the invitation to hold meetings in London. They had finished well in New York and decided to let the closure come. I was so proud of my father. His strength had held. The response to the gospel had been powerful. And God had given Daddy the opportunity to complete the work. That by itself — the chance to finish — was a gift. Nearly sixty years of crusade ministry ended beautifully, with joy and the move of God in the lives of people — the people of the world. For the whole world can be found at the crossroads that is New York, as my father said in his press conference. At his last crusade, he literally was able to love the world.

As I write this, Daddy is at home working on a new book and trying to maintain his health. He still walks up and down the driveway — not the steep hill, but a small slope — going out with his walker a couple of times a day, staying disciplined with his exercise. He tries to eat well and rest a good deal, and he is even considering a preaching date in New Orleans.

When I look at my father now, I see a man at peace; there is a tranquility about him. I know he gets frustrated with the aging process, with his limitations; but it is as if the wisdom of the ages has settled on him, and he is at rest. I have encouraged him to write a book about growing old — to share the ways God continues to be faithful even as the body declines. These latter years have been challenging for Daddy. He is a man of vision, and he realizes he will not see all of the vision come to pass. He has had to hand his life's work over to another. That has not been easy — nor would it be for any man. But my father has placed his faith in God, as he has done for a lifetime; and God has been faithful. Daddy is grateful knowing the ministry will continue, and through it all, he has arrived at a place of lasting peace. He is in God's hands, as he has said.

My father talked about his peace at the New York press conference and during media interviews surrounding the crusade, sharing an experience he had several years ago while going into brain surgery at Mayo's. He recently shared the story again around the dinner table when my son asked him about growing older.

In 2000, doctors determined my father was not suffering from Parkinson's disease but from hydrocephalus, a condition caused by too much fluid on the brain. Daddy was advised to have a shunt put into his brain to drain the fluid off; unfortunately, the surgery had to be performed three times. One night, as Daddy readied himself for the operation, he felt as if he were dying. In that moment, he says, all of his sins — a lifetime of sins, even from his childhood — marched before him. Seeing the sins, my father turned to the Lord in his heart, by faith, and instantly felt an overwhelming peace come over him — and the realization that he was totally forgiven, forgiven for every sin. At the press conference, Daddy explained that the peace he experienced then was the greatest peace he has ever known. And one he has never lost.

"I'm thankful for the peace of God in my heart," he told the media gathered at Rockefeller Center, "and that could happen to everybody — whatever your problem, whatever your need, Jesus can come into your heart and forgive you and guarantee to you life in this life, but [also] life beyond this life."

Listening to my father, I thought, here is a man who sees his whole life — everything about it, every experience, thought, and challenge — as material he can use to show others what is available to them in Christ. His story of God's peace, of his intimate moment in prayer when he thought he was dying, he shared with the whole world. Something about my father's transparency here gets to the heart of who he is. Having given his life to God, Daddy allows God to use the stuff of his life, even his most private moments, to bring hope to people and show them the way to God's love. My father isn't holding back or holding on to anything. He trusts God completely. That is where peace is — and it is where I long to be.

THE LITTLE PLATFORM

In between periods of rest, my father continues to follow world news. As he told the New York audience, he reads several papers at breakfast, trying to keep up with what's happening. In one message he noted that news reporters had been asking him about the condition of the world: "What's wrong with our world?" they wanted to know. "What's happening?" Daddy gave the audience his answer. "The Bible says that our problem is sin." And he carried it on from there, sharing the solution — Jesus. As he said at the press conference, "I believe that the gospel of Christ is the answer, not part of the answer but the whole answer. We don't have any possibility of solving our problems today except through Jesus."

As I have shared, my father became especially ardent following world events two months after the New York crusade as Hurricane Katrina swept away New Orleans and wrecked the Gulf Coast. When I went home to Montreat shortly afterward, Daddy could talk of nothing else. Overwhelmed by the devastation and the needs, he couldn't tear himself away from the television. What could he do? He gave money. But he couldn't go down to the coast and see the damage and touch people's lives as he had done in the wake of other natural disasters. He told me he felt helpless, and I could see the frustration in his face. In a public statement, he said the Katrina disaster "may be the worst tragedy America has known since the Civil War."[3]

Then my parents saw an opportunity to do something on what might be considered a small scale, hoping churches across the country would follow suit: they "adopted" a family displaced by the storm and loaned them the house they own — the "Old House," where we used to live — at the bottom of the mountain in Montreat.

Franklin had met the family at a shelter in Shreveport, Louisiana, and was moved by their story. Based in New Orleans, the Medrano family had stuck out the storm first in a hotel and then in a Catholic church before they were finally rescued by boat. Three generations were represented by the five family members; the oldest, Ernestina Martinez, a native of Honduras, was in her late seventies. She had been hurt trying to swim through rushing floodwaters filled with debris.

On a recent visit to Montreat, I had the opportunity to meet the family; I walked into the Old House during one of Daddy's visits with them. Mrs. Martinez was talking as I entered the living room. Daddy sat next to her on the couch, holding her hand. She was speaking softly in Spanish, and a translator knelt in front of them, sharing Mrs. Martinez's story in English with Daddy and his associates.

My father listened intently. I hoped he wasn't having trouble hearing — he seemed to nod at the appropriate times as Mrs. Martinez talked of being injured by debris while swimming for her life in the floodwaters. The late afternoon light was streaming through the windows, and after awhile, as the conversation was winding down, Daddy said, "Let me pray for you."

I looked at my father sitting there on the couch, holding Mrs. Martinez's hand, and I thought about the times he had led us in family devotions here in this very room when I was a little girl. My first childhood memory is of kneeling by the fireplace in the Old House during family devotions and fiddling with a loose brick on the hearth while the adults prayed. Now some fifty years later, Daddy was still praying here.

Listening as my father began to speak, giving the translator time to relay in Spanish what he was saying, I realized that as Daddy prayed, he was giving the gospel. He thanked Jesus for dying on the cross. Then he said, "Thank you that we

DADDY WITH MRS. MARTINEZ

can accept you as our Lord and Savior, thank you that you give us eternal life." He was making sure that his guests knew the gospel. My father was preaching, even in his prayers. He was being himself at home, as authentic as ever, loving those in his midst.

The big platform might be gone, I thought, standing there in the Old House looking on. The vast crowds, the arenas — the time for that is over now. But the little platform, the one-on-one, is still available to Daddy. And he will use it for God. As long as he is with us he will use it. Because that is who he is.

Daddy with the Medrano family, Montreat 2005

# A Tribute to My Father

These past months I have sensed a crowd gathering at Heaven's gate in anticipation of my father's arrival. What excitement and eager anticipation on both sides. As the book title says, "Heaven is for real." And for those who have put their faith in Jesus as their Savior, Heaven is where we will spend eternity. My father will be there.

My youngest daughter says she would love to be a fly on the wall (surely there are no flies in Heaven!) when her Daddy Bill meets Jesus. I thought about that. My father has been walking with Jesus for so many years . . . I imagine they will hug deeply as Jesus whispers, "Well done, my good and faithful servant." It will be a brother greeting a brother, a Father welcoming His son . . . the familiarity had long ago been established.

And no doubt, it will be a battle-scarred warrior returning from the front to lay his victory at the feet of his King amid great celebration. The warrior claims no honor for himself but gives it all to his King. Many have commented on my father's great humility. It is because he understands his mission—it was not to amass the world's acclaim or admiration or fame. It was not to gain wealth—that was one of his fears. It was to do his Lord's bidding. It was not to build *a* kingdom but *The* Kingdom.

So many have commented to me that my father's reward will be huge in Heaven. No doubt it will be. But perhaps not as we would reward—for the vast crowds that came to hear him preach or the thousands who responded to the invitation to receive Christ. God doesn't see things as we do. God rewards faithfulness, not numbers. My father will be rewarded for his faithfulness just as the fireman who showed up day after day, or the nurse, or the teacher, or the janitor. No matter what our task, when we do it as unto the Lord faithfully, day after day, whether we feel like it or not, God sees and God will reward us.

The big change is that my father will no longer have limitations. His body will be strong and young again. All the travelling and preaching took its toll—for years. He said he never felt the same after the 1957 New York Crusade in Madison Square Garden. The reunion with family members will be sweet since here on earth he was so often unavailable to them. I hope God gives my mother and father 1,000 years to be alone and enjoy each other. (There was never any privacy here on earth.)

People have speculated about my father's wealth and imagined a fortune. Things never interested my father. He

lives comfortably but simply for a man of his stature. Though some would consider him a celebrity, he considers himself a simple farm boy from North Carolina. His tastes are simple. He loves hotdogs and beans out of a can. He is easy to please. After my mother died, we went to the house to begin the process of sorting things out. We went room to room. When we got to my father's room there was very little of value, only sentiment: books, photos, childish drawings from great-grandchildren—not much of worldly value. My sister, Anne, looked around the room slowly and said, "A man of God values little the things of the world." My father is a man of God.

Is he perfect? No! He can be short—we knew those steely eyes and set jaw meant the discussion was over! Our lives were impacted by his long absences and his preoccupation and distraction when he was home. Because of schedules and staff there was little intimacy with our Daddy. We took it when we could get it.

But now he is preparing to enter the Presence of the One he serves. We will rejoice when the time comes, knowing that he fought a good fight; he finished his course; he kept the faith and there awaits for him a crown of righteousness.

We will miss him. Most of us have never known a world without him. In a world bereft of courageous, true, honorable men—he is one. I have been blessed to call him "Daddy."

N Bánya

Monsieur

Bela Székula 9012

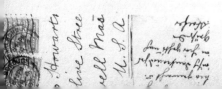

# ENDNOTES

CHAPTER 1

1.  Billy Graham, *Just As I Am: The Autobiography of Billy Graham*
    (San Francisco: HarperSanFrancisco/Zondervan, 1997), 565.
2.  Ibid 702-703

CHAPTER 3

1.  Graham, *Just As I Am*, 723.
2.  Ibid, 324
3.  Russ Busby, *Billy Graham: God's Ambassador*
    (Charlotte, NC: Billy Graham Evangelical Association, 1999), 93.
4.  Graham, *Just As I Am*, 324.
5.  Ibid., 421
6.  Billy Graham, *"The Role of Religion in American Society,"* (paper presented at
    Nanjing University, Nanjing, 21 April 1988), Private sermon collection,
    Montreat, NC.

CHAPTER 4

1.  Ruth Bell Graham, *It's My Turn*
    (Old Tappan, New Jersey: Fleming H. Revell Company, 1982), 62.
2.  Graham, *Just As I Am*, 212.

CHAPTER 5

1.  Graham, *Just As I Am*, 28.
2.  George W. Bush, *A Charge to Keep*
    (New York: William Morrow and Company Inc. 1999), 136.

3. Patricia Daniels Cornwell, *A Time for Remembering: The Ruth Bell Graham Story* (San Francisco: Harper & Row, 1983), 217.

4. Graham, *Just As I Am*, 135.

5. Ibid, 138.

6. Ibid, 138-139.

7. Ibid, 139.

8. Ibid, 139.

9. Ibid, 137.

CHAPTER 6

1. Graham, *Just As I Am*, 324.

2. Harold Myra and Marshall Shelley, *The Leadership Secrets of Billy Graham,* (Grand Rapids MI: Zondervan, 2005), 317

3. "Statement by Billy Graham on Hurricane Katrina" *Billy Graham Evangelistic Association* http://www.bgea.com/News_Article.asp?ArtivleID=112 (February 14, 2006)

# PHOTO CREDITS

Cover: Photograph by Russ Busby

## CHAPTER 1

Page 6: Photograph by Russ Busby
Page 12: Photograph by Luverne Gustavson
Page 15: Photograph by Russ Busby
Page 18: Photograph by Luverne Gustavson
Page 19: Photograph by Tom Blau
Page 24: Photograph by Tom Blau
Page 34–35: Photographs by Russ Busby

## CHAPTER 2

Page 41: Photograph by Ned Graham
Page 44: Photograph by Russ Busby
Page 58–59: Photographs by Russ Busby
Page 63: Photograph by Russ Busby

## CHAPTER 3

Page 64: Photograph by Russ Busby
Page 68–69: Photographs by Russ Busby
Page 72–73: Photographs by Russ Busby

Page 175: Photograph by Russ Busby
Page 179: Photograph by Russ Busby
Page 185: Photograph by Russ Busby
Page 188–189: Photographs by Maury Scobee

Other photographs are from Ruth's personal collection.

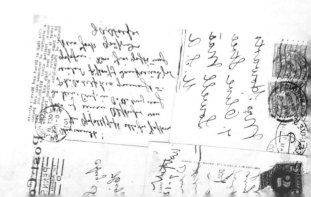